THE BEST OF BRITISH BUSES

Nº7 AEC REGENTS
1929 - 1942

ALAN TOWNSIN

TITLES IN THIS SERIES

First Published by Transport Publishing Company Ltd November 1982
This book exclusively reprinted for BOOKLAW/RAILBUS TRANSPORT EDITIONS June 1993

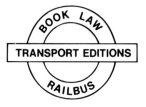

Designed, typeset and produced for the Publishers by
Mopok Graphics, 128 Pikes Lane, Glossop, Derbyshire
Printed and bound in Great Britain

Contents

FRONT COVER ILLUSTRATION
Brighton Corporation's first motor buses, placed in service in Spring 1939, were built at a time when Regent buyers were offered an exceptional range of preferences. The newly-appointed General Manager of the transport undertaking, Mr Winston Robinson, chose what amounted to a double-decker version of the contemporary Green Line coach for the 21 Regent chassis, with 8.8-litre direct-injection engine and preselective gearbox. Weymann's standard body style of the period suited them well. The author was able to make closer acquaintance with No. 63, better known by its registration number FUF 63, when it had been purchased for preservation by Michael Dryhurst, and shared in driving it to Halifax in 1968, including a surprisingly enjoyable trip across London. This photograph was taken at Brighton after arrival on the annual Historic Commercial Vehicle Run the same year — in the background is the author's Riley 2½-litre car, still owned and itself now 30 years old.

Introduction

In one sense, it probably seemed to some outside observers that AEC could hardly fail with a new double-decker in 1929, with the London General Omnibus Co as a 'captive' market. In fact, the LGOC management tended to view AEC, despite its origins as simply their company's vehicle-manufacturing offshoot, as rather a precocious child. But Lord Ashfield, Chairman of the Underground group to which both firms belonged, saw the need to strengthen AEC's position as a manufacturer, and had attracted John Rackham from Leyland to do just that.

Like the Regal, the Regent had the problem of competing against Leyland's equivalent model, which Rackham had created two years earlier and which was even more strongly entrenched in the double-decker market than the corresponding Tiger was among single-deckers. The Regent was able to offer some practical advantages — a more compact front-end and such important details as easier access to the sparking plugs. It also had the goodwill associated with previous AEC double-deckers — outclassed by the Titan, but hitherto respected, if in a more limited market of potential users.

As it turned out, the Regent performed so well in LGOC service as to sweep away all doubts as to its suitability. For a time, the LGOC reverted to its attraction to the six-wheeler, and so the Renown model of this layout, rather unwillingly created by Rackham but the most successful of such vehicles, took the major share of LGOC's requirements for 1931 and 1932. But the 800-odd Regents delivered in 1930 and the early months of 1931 forming the ST class, were appreciably cheaper to operate and the possibility of getting as many passengers into an extended version as could be accommodated in the LGOC Renowns had obvious appeal. When slightly longer chassis appeared at the end of 1931, the implications were obvious and even though it was not until the end of 1932 that the LGOC got its 60-seat version out, the Regent thereafter never looked back.

Meanwhile, several technical innovations were taking place, and though these were largely developed on LGOC's Renown buses, the know-how put AEC in a strong position. Oil engines — they were rarely referred to as 'diesels' in Britain in those days — were a case in point, and although apt to be troublesome at first, AEC was able to offer a well-proved unit by 1932, when Leyland's equivalent was barely out of the experimental stage.

Lord Ashfield and John Rackham can share the credit for obtaining the rights for AEC to use the Daimler combination of fluid flywheel and Wilson-type preselective epicyclic gearbox. This was to prove the most successful transmission for urban buses, certainly in Britain, in the 'thirties and indeed was the basis for the most widely used systems on British buses half a century later. Daimler's own chassis was not at first very competitive, mainly due to engine design limitations, and by the mid-'thirties there were more gearboxes of this type in AEC chassis, mainly Regents, than in Daimler despite the latter's standardisation on this form of transmission.

From the middle 'thirties, however, Daimler was offering effective competition with its Gardner-engined models. Leyland had also strengthened its already powerful position with a compact 8.6-litre direct-injection oil engine, widely adopted in both company and municipal fleets. Its torque converter transmission was attracting a good deal of attention among urban operators, even if Daimler and AEC's fluid flywheel and Wilson gearbox combination was to win this sales battle, particularly important when re-training tram drivers for bus work, in the long run.

The year 1932 was one which brought a wider range of options as well as changes to the standard Regent specification. This example on chassis number 6611907, one of those for the Belfast Omnibus Co Ltd, had the recently introduced 16ft. 3in. wheelbase and 120 bhp 'high power head' 7.4-litre petrol engine, both standard by that date, and also fluid transmission, with preselective gearbox supplied by Daimler. Weymann built the timber-framed body to a design also supplied to several English companies. It is seen at Bangor in company with a contemporary Austin Seven saloon, shortly before BOC was taken over by the newly-formed Northern Ireland Road Transport Board in 1935.

Had it not been for massive London Transport orders, the Regent sales position would not have looked particularly impressive around 1934, but the 7.7-litre engine, especially in direct-injection form, helped to broaden the model's appeal. The policy towards the end of the 'thirties of offering a wide variety of specifications may have arisen almost accidentally, but it undoubtedly helped overall sales. The development of the RT, in response to London Transport's far-seeing specification for a double-decker setting new standards of refinement and durability, could be counted as an investment for the future.

The outbreak of war in September 1939 came before that line of development could get into its stride. It is interesting to speculate what might have happened had peace continued — some rationalisation of the range appears to have been inevitable. However, the war years undoubtedly gave a useful opportunity to sort out what was at first a rather troublesome brake system on the RT which might have discouraged the British bus industry's almost universal adoption of air-pressure brake systems, in which AEC was a market leader, in the early post-war years.

As it turned out, the Regents produced in 1941-42 were built to a standardised specification, so the wheel had turned through a full circle back to what amounted to a single model policy. But overall, much of the fascination of the Regents of 1929-42 lay in their variety, as I hope this volume will convey.

Basingstoke, 1982   Alan Townsin

This front view of the prototype Regent chassis, taken shortly after completion in the winter of 1928-29, shows a close approximation to the appearance of the production Regent that was to remain virtually unchanged until 1937. The radiator grille outline on the first dozen chassis was slightly different to the later standard and the typically 'twenties-style tyres are another giveaway, but the essentials are all there. Note the offset engine position as shown by the starting handle and sump.

Chapter One: Rackham's rescue bid.

Progress in bus design was exceptionally rapid in Britain in the late 'twenties. By 1928 both the London General Omnibus Co Ltd and its vehicle-manufacturing subsidiary, the Associated Equipment Co Ltd, had lost the lead in city bus development which had been theirs only a couple of years earlier. Moreover, they were in some difficulties in trying to retrieve the position. This situation was by no means entirely their own fault for officialdom had held back the fruits of their efforts to produce a low-loading covered-top double-decker, the NS-type, which could have gone into production in 1923 but did not enter service in the intended form in any quantity until the Spring of 1926. Soon there were over 2,000 on London's streets,

but even by then there was a need to catch up with fresh thinking on such subjects as pneumatic tyres.

Attention had subsequently been concentrated on a six-wheeled double-decker, the LS, introduced with enthusiasm in May 1927. However, only 20 were built in 1927-28, of which a mere dozen entered service with the LGOC. Six-wheeled buses were distinctly fashionable at the time, but possibly the biggest step forward in the progress of the double-decker motor bus during the whole of its career had materialised in 1927. This was the introduction of an altogether bolder design of two-axle double-decker than anything seen before. This was the original Titan TD1 model announced by Leyland Motors Ltd, together with the

corresponding Tiger single-decker. In those days this concern had no connection with AEC or, indeed, any other bus manufacturer and competition for business was intense. The Titan immediately attracted numerous orders including some particularly prestigious ones, such as that for 100 vehicles for Glasgow Corporation.

It had been hoped that a link-up between AEC and Daimler that had been set up in 1926 would enable vehicles made at AEC's new works at Southall to be sold on a much larger scale than hitherto. The Associated Daimler Co Ltd was the organisation created for this purpose, and the vehicles were sold under the ADC name for a couple of years. However, this was not working out too well

and by the beginning of 1928 some ADC single-deck models were being built at the Daimler works in Coventry. No model that could hope to compete with the Titan was available from within the failing ADC empire.

However, Lord Ashfield, who was both Chairman of the Underground group of companies, of which both LGOC and hence AEC were subsidiaries, and was also Chairman of ADC, was never a man to let grass grow under his feet. At the same time as revealing in July 1928 that AEC and Daimler would henceforth go their separate ways, he was able to announce the appointment as AEC's Chief Engineer of George John Rackham, the very man who had created the major threat to the plans for expanding bus production at Southall, for he had designed the Titan, having been Leyland's Chief Engineer for two years.

Rackham's career and the ADC story are covered more fully in 'Blue Triangle', the author's history of AEC and its buses. However, it is worth mentioning that he had been Chief Draughtsman at the Walthamstow works which had been AEC's earlier home from 1911 to 1916 and indeed his connection with LGOC went back to 1907. He had spent four years in the United States as Chief Engineer of the Yellow Coach Manufacturing Co Ltd in Chicago from 1922 until he went to Leyland. Lord Ashfield, whose early career had also included a period in the United States, was sufficiently interested in Rackham's ideas to have chosen a Yellow Y-type for his personal 9-seat parlour coach delivered in 1927.

Lord Ashfield realised the potential of being able to find a truly competitive bus range to produce at Southall, not only for use by LGOC but also for sale to the rapidly expanding market, not least to other cities and com-

panies whose interest in double-deck buses as the answer to their rolling stock needs, was growing fast, often as a replacement for tramway systems.

So Rackham's brief was clear. Create a range of AEC buses to compete effectively with the new Leylands. The author has been told that his salary was some £6,000 per annum, an almost fabulous sum in those days, making him the highest paid man on the premises. Such a sum would be greater in today's terms than those paid nowadays to the very top people in the biggest firms in the British motor industry. Such comparisons are probably misleading in the very different circumstances of the times, but if generously rewarded, he immediately set about a course of action which was to make immensely greater sums for AEC.

The first step was the development of a new engine, the prototype of which was running by the end of September 1928. This was the famous 6-type and even had it been an exact copy of the Titan's power unit, such speed in completion would be regarded as phenomenal nowadays. It was certainly similar in general concept, with six cylinders and overhead camshaft layout, and in many detail features. However, it differed in dimensions — AEC, like several firms in the motor industry in those days, used metric dimensions and the bore and stroke were 100 mm and 130 mm respectively instead of the Leyland's 4in. by 5½in., producing an engine of slightly smaller swept volume, 6.1 litres instead of 6.8 litres. However, the shorter stroke enabled it to run at slightly higher speed and the power output, 95 bhp, was much the same. This was an increase of some 66 per cent on the output of the final version of the four-cylinder engine fitted to the NS-type, so performance was greatly im-

proved. Even more dramatic was the improvement in the standard of refinement — the Rackham-designed six-cylinder petrol engines were almost inaudible when idling and remained smooth throughout the speed range.

An engine was fitted to an existing 416-model single-decker for experimental purposes and in January 1929, the first model having the 6-type engine was announced. This was the Reliance, model 660, which was in effect the 416 chassis, with the 'face-lift' improvements in appearance which had been introduced the previous year as model 426 and no more than minor modifications to accept the new engine. No double-decker version was offered and the Reliance of this era was no more than a stop-gap, albeit an unusually successful one, to prop up AEC sales until the new range of chassis which Rackham had put in hand could be offered. More on the model appears in 'Blue Triangle' and the companion volume 'Best of British Buses No. 6 — AEC Regal'.

Three versions of the completely new range of chassis were being developed, and a clue to the relative importance given to them by Rackham is given by the order of the model numbers allocated. The first was to be type 661, a two-axle double-decker given the type name Regent, the others being 662, the corresponding Regal single-decker, and 663, which was a three-axle chassis, designed to meet continuing LGOC interest in six-wheel double-deckers. Rackham had never disguised his preference for the four-wheeler (or if one is to be pedantic, the two-axle chassis with twin wheels and tyres on the rear axle) and his faith that the six-wheeled bus would prove to be but a passing fashion. However, it was not until 1933 that the LGOC was entirely convinced, and indeed there was

The rivals. Leyland's new Titan TD1 model made an immense impact on the bus industry. By about September 1928, when this photograph was taken, delivery was in hand of an order for 100 examples for Glasgow Corporation which had followed an initial batch of thirteen supplied earlier in the year. The four vehicles shown, Glasgow numbers 109-111 and another unidentified bus from the same order, illustrate the characteristic lines of the standard Leyland bodywork, of patented lowbridge design.

a curious state of scepticism in LGOC's overall attitude to its AEC offspring's latest ventures — LGOC's own drawing office was working independently on its own new bus designs.

The first Regent chassis was evidently completed before the end of December 1928, again remarkably quickly for a design that had virtually nothing in common with previous AEC practice. The specification and many features of the detail design were strongly reminiscent of the Leyland TD1, though again the actual dimensions were different, the wheelbase being nearly a foot shorter at 15ft. 6½in., though the overall length was the same at 25ft. The single-plate clutch was given plenty of lining area and had a smooth action, doubtless being designed to

stand up to the rigours of repeated stops and restarts in London service. The gearbox was not exactly silent, being inferior in this respect to the chain gearboxes used on most NS models and earlier LGOC chassis, but had an instantly recognisable and, to the author at any rate, rather agreeable whine which could rise to quite an exciting scream if the bus was driven with sufficient enthusiasm.

The chassis layout, with relatively low frame height achieved by a gracefully curved profile over the front and rear axles and offset transmission line, was very much in the tradition of both the Titan TD1 and Rackham's Yellow Y-type. The single-servo brake system and Marles steering were also in the Titan tradition, but the front-end layout and

appearance were quite different. In one sense, they conformed more closely to previous AEC ideas on compact design, for this tradition went back to the K-type of 1919 that had very largely set the pattern for the typical British half-cab bus. The idea of mounting the radiator well forward to line up with the front of the frame had appeared on the S-type at the end of 1920, and in this sense most AEC models of the 'twenties were tidier than the TD1 with its projecting dumb-irons.

However, the final touch of artistry — for, like many famous engineers, Rackham undoubtedly had an artist's eye — was the radiator design. Entirely new, it was of more slender proportions than most of its contemporaries, and with the front grille extending over almost its full

This unfamiliar view of the 6-type engine, as mounted in the prototype Regent chassis, shows how 'clean' the offside of the modern-looking six-cylinder engine was, with nothing requiring regular attention above cab floor level. Note also how the radiator was supported from the engine and the layout of the driver's controls, setting the standard pattern for numerous later designs. Early Regents had Marles steering gear very like that used on the Titan and recognisable from the AEC-manufactured worm-and-nut type introduced in 1931 by the absence of the enlarged column diameter just under the steering wheel required to house the top bearing of the latter unit.

When the first official photographs of the bodied prototype Regent, 661001, by then registered MT 2114, were taken early in 1929, the resemblance of the bodywork to the contemporary Leyland standard body for the Titan was obvious, particularly as it was, no doubt deliberately, photographed from a position which did not reveal the humped 'camel' roof cross-section. Short Bros had built the 50-seat body to AEC's design, which followed Leyland practice even in such details as the sidelamp position. However, the Regent chassis front-end was quite different, setting a fresh standard for others, including eventually Leyland, to follow.

depth, it set new standards of style, making most existing designs look dated. The AEC bullseye monogram was enclosed in a triangular badge outline which had appeared on the Reliance, but now it was an integral part of the design.

It was evidently decided that a dozen Regents would be produced initially and most of these were to be fitted with a body designed by AEC but, as AEC never had its own body-building facilities, this initial batch was entrusted to Short Bros of Rochester. The styling again showed evidence of Rackham influence, and indeed the overall resemblance to the standard TD1 body was obvious, save in one important respect. Leyland's side-gangway lowbridge layout was patented and the AEC version was a centre-gangway design but with the so-called camel roof cross-section, giving an illusion

of similarly low build — a psychological factor when double-deckers were still rare in many areas. The piano-front profile was reminiscent both of the standard TD1 body and Yellow double-deckers. At the rear, the open staircase was normal practice for the period, though soon to be upstaged by Leyland's enclosed staircase version of the TD1 body introduced in the later summer of 1929.

The first chassis, numbered 661001, received the first example of this body style, which seated 26 passengers upstairs and 24 downstairs. It was registered in Middlesex, for use as an AEC demonstrator and thus became MT 2114, a number which suggests a date before the end of 1928, MT issues having begun in August of that year and being completed by June 1929, though Middlesex was apt to be a little erratic.

AEC records showed the date of delivery as 13th February 1929 — it was probably complete with body at that date. After demonstration duties all over the country, latterly in the livery of Glasgow Corporation, it was delivered to Halifax Corporation on 17th February 1930.

However, the record for the second chassis, 661002, is more explicit. It was delivered to the National Omnibus & Transport Co Ltd at that concern's Colchester branch on 12th April 1929. It had the same type of bodywork and was registered VW 9565, receiving the fleet number 2902. No public announcement of the model had been made at this stage, nor indeed until after all this initial dozen had been delivered.

The third chassis was to go considerably further afield. Records show that it was ordered in March 1929 by Anglo-Argentine Tramways Co

ARRANGEMENT OF AEC REGENT CHASSIS

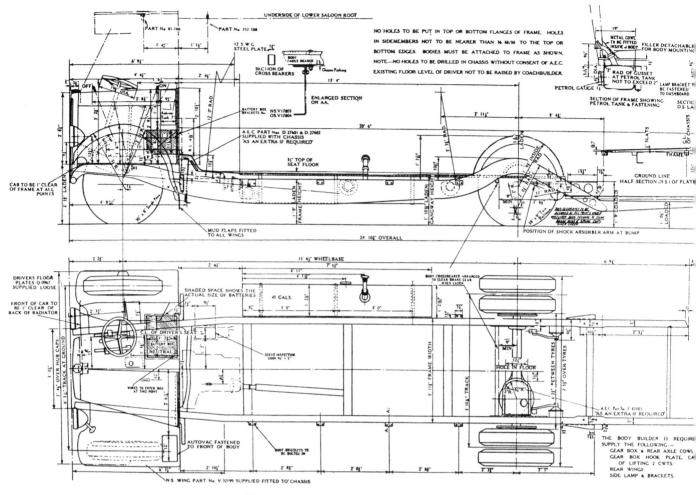

These drawings are reproduced from the original AEC Regent catalogue of October 1929 to a scale of 7 mm to 1ft. The body cross-sections were not identified, but probably refer to the Hall, Lewis low-height and normal-height designs of the time.

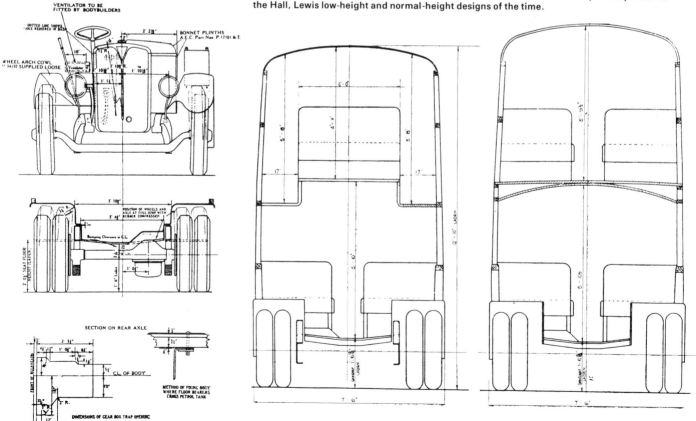

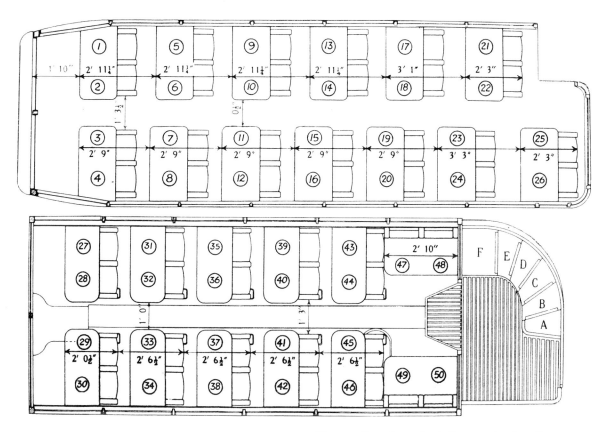

These seating plans, also to 7 mm scale, show the arrangement, with 26 seats upstairs and 24 downstairs, used on the original AEC-design body as built for early Regents.

Ltd of Buenos Aires, a British-owned concern and already a major AEC customer, with 110 NS-type chassis bodied as single-deckers. 661003 was shipped to Agar Cross & Co Ltd, the AEC agents in Buenos Aires on 13th May 1929. However, it was returned to Britain and delivered to L. R. Mansfield, of Leytonstone in July 1931 for use as a furniture van, a body of this type being built by the operator.

Chassis 661004 with standard Short Bros AEC-design body was supplied to Thomas Tilling Ltd in June 1929, being registered UU 9161. Although Tilling was soon to be a major Regent customer, this initial vehicle was not retained for long, being returned to AEC and used for staff transport in July 1930 and being transferred to the oddly-named Walthamstow Wayfarers Club in March 1931, later being sold and rebodied as a single-decker. In those days transport of workers from the area of the old Walthamstow works was carried out on quite a large scale.

Chassis numbers 661005, 661006 and 661007, again with Short Bros bodies of the same type, were all delivered to the National Omnibus & Transport Co Ltd in June 1929. Of these, 661006 joined 661002, being numbered 2903 and registered in Essex as VX 895. The other two were allocated to the Dorset area, being numbered 2905 and 2904

and registered TK 3024 and 3023 respectively. At the time, the National concern was in process of splitting its operating activities into separate companies and thus the Essex-registered vehicles passed to the Eastern National Omnibus Co Ltd in 1930 and the Dorset-registered pair to Southern National. Except for 2903, withdrawn after an accident in 1939, they had long careers with these operators, surviving until 1954 albeit rebodied as indicated in a later chapter.

The first Regent to be supplied to an LGOC-related fleet was 661008, delivered to the East Surrey Traction Co Ltd, in those days LGOC's principal 'country' offshoot in July 1929. It was given one of a batch of registration numbers that had been reserved by the LGOC, UU 6610, though it never came into central London service. This was because of the body design — again the standard AEC-pattern Short Bros production. The vehicle had a somewhat complex career, being operated for a time by Autocar Services Ltd of Tunbridge Wells, apparently from October 1929, though it later came into ESTC's own fleet as No. 255. Although the formation of London Transport brought it into this organisation's fleet, it did not receive a 'London' fleet number until 1935 when it became ST1139, thus having the highest ST number although the oldest representative of that class.

It remained in service as a green-painted country bus with original body, latterly somewhat modified, until 1948.

The first Regents for municipal operators were delivered in July 1929. Of these, 661009, with standard AEC-design Short Bros body, went to Wallasey Corporation. AEC records suggest that it returned to AEC, the dates November 1929 and January 1930 being also quoted under the heading 'delivered', the latter with the note "off float". It seems that several, possibly all, of these early vehicles were initially supplied on some form of trial basis. However, Wallasey did add 661009 to its permanent fleet, retaining it until March 1938, not a long life by later standards but well up to average expectations in 1929.

Some form of 'sale or return' agreement certainly applied to 661010 and 011, supplied to Birmingham Corporation Tramways and Omnibus Department also in July 1929. Although they were the first two of a batch of 30, the chassis (which had been registered OF 3970 and 3971) were returned to AEC in June 1930 and two new chassis, 661764/5 supplied (the latter being registered OG 3639/8 and receiving the bodies and fleet numbers 339/8 from the 1929 chassis). The body-work on these 30 vehicles was of a new pattern, with somewhat exag-

To add to the publicity surrounding the announcement of the Regent in October 1929, the first vehicle, 661001 [MT 2114], still in original demonstration livery, was taken to Brooklands Racing Track, where it is seen storming up the 1 in 4 test hill. The famous banked track is visible in the background and on the left a shed occupied by Vickers Ltd, ultimately to take over the whole of the site during the 1939-45 war, bringing the race track to an end.

The more important part of the visit of MT 2114 was a twelve-hour 500-mile continuous run. This implies an average speed of 41.6 mph, which would still be no mean achievement for a double-decker half-a-century later. The original caption to this picture from the first Regent catalogue reads "Rounding the bank at 50 miles per hour". The standard rear axle ratio of 6.25 to 1 would just about have permitted a 1 in 4 gradient capability and such a top speed, which would have represented 2,950 engine rpm. Such an engine speed was possible with the 6-type engine, for which a speed range of 300 to 3,000 rpm was sometimes quoted. The standard peak engine power of 95 bhp was developed at 2,500 rpm with "an economical road setting" of the carburetter, according to the same catalogue, which suggests that the engine may have been tuned to give a little more power for the Brooklands run. Even so, 50 mph was as much as a typical small car of the day could manage, flat out.

gerated piano-front and enclosed stairs, that was to set the standard for Birmingham's Regents of the period up to 1931, though later versions were more modern-looking in such aspects as roof contour. The returned chassis found new homes, 661010 going to Clayton Dewandre in January 1931, presumably for use on brake development, while 661011 was sent to Short Bros in July 1930, presumably for a new body and then had a spell with AEC as demonstrator or works transport until it was transferred to the Walthamstow Wayfarer fleet in April 1931 — later it became a single-decker in independent operators' fleets.

The final chassis of the dozen was recorded in AEC service records as going to Hall, Lewis for a covered-top double-deck body apparently in June 1930 and then running for AEC until going to the Walthamstow Wayfarers fleet in March 1931. In fact, other evidence confirms that this bus was bodied by the Summer of 1929; it was to be the low-height demonstrator in Glasgow colours and was registered GE 6326.

The National Omnibus & Transport Co Ltd
was the first operator to add a Regent to its
fleet, when 661002 was delivered to its
Colchester branch in April 1929, receiving
the fleet number 2902 and being registered
VW 9565. This photograph was evidently
taken when it returned to Southall briefly
around July of that year [with tyres noticeably worn], by which time NOTC had received three more of the preliminary batch
of a dozen Regents, 661005, 661006 and
661007, all with the standard AEC-design
50-seat Short Bros body. No doubt such parts
as the mudguards were hand made, which
probably accounts for the noticeably more
domed front nearside wing seen on No. 2902.
This evidently survived at least until July
1938 when the smaller photograph was
taken, showing this vehicle with, partly
visible on the left, 661006 [fleet number
2903]. By this date the NOTC's East Anglian
business had become the Eastern National
Omnibus Co Ltd. Although 2902 had evidently lost its front registration plate from
the later-type standard radiator by then
fitted, it survived with ENOC until 1954,
having been rebodied by East Lancashire in
1944, and fitted with 7.7-litre oil engine
at about the same date. No. 2903 was less
fortunate, being withdrawn after an accident
in 1939, the only one of the four not to survive until 1954 as the two others, latterly
with Southern National, were also rebodied,
in this case by Beadle, and thus also ran for
a quarter century like 661002 — a remarkable age especially for pre-production
vehicles. The Leyland Lion on the right of
the picture, a PLSC3 model, was only
slightly older, dating from 1928 and having
a Strachan & Brown body.

Regents 661004-009 were all delivered in June-July 1929 and all had the AEC-design Short Bros open-staircase body, though with minor variations. Two were clearly intended to meet Metropolitan Police requirements, with rather clumsy-looking brackets for a large London-style route board at front and rear and route number holders on the sides as well as the front. They also had open-sided cabs, although they were provided with glass windscreens and a slender pillar on the offside gave an illusion of a conventional quarter window. Chassis 661004 was supplied to Thomas Tilling Ltd as that Company's number 6000 in June 1929, being registered UU 9161, as shown above. Chassis number 661008 was officially lent to and licensed by the LGOC, receiving the registration number UU 6610 [immediately preceding that of the first Renown which was given the fleet number LT1 and registered UU 6611],

but was delivered in July 1929 to LGOC's 'country' subsidiary, the East Surrey Traction Co Ltd, based at Bell Street, Reigate, having been painted in that concern's livery, as shown below.

It is clear that the body design did not meet with approval for London service. The 'camel' roof may have given a 'lowbridge' appearance to a normal-height bus but it gave reduced headroom over the seats on the upper-deck, particularly those near the windows. Although Tilling soon placed an order for some 136 Regents for service in London and Brighton delivered in 1930, number 6000 was not retained. LGOC had its own quite different ideas on body design and any hopes at Southall that the AEC body might be adopted as a standard in London as well as elsewhere were immediately dashed, despite favourable reaction to the chassis.

It was not long before 661008 [UU 6610] lost its original East Surrey identity and moved on in October 1929 to Autocar Services Ltd of Tunbridge Wells, also at that time part of the LGOC empire [and having Bell Street, Reigate as its official address], for a three-month spell, at that stage still on loan. Its seating capacity was 51, with 27 upstairs and 24 down. In December 1929 it was officially taken into LGOC stock but allocated once more to East Surrey, becoming No. 255, remaining in this fleet until it was reformed as London General Country Services Ltd, which concern did not use fleet numbers. When London Transport took over LGCS, the resulting country department still did not use fleet numbers. It was not until maintenance was brought under the control of Chiswick that they were allocated to vehicles that had not had LGOC numbers on a basis of alphabetical order of registration marks. This produced the ironic effect that the oldest London Regent received the highest fleet number in the ST series, ST1139 [other than the first RT — see p. 70].

The first municipal Regent was 661009, delivered to Wallasey Corporation in July 1929. This had the standard 'provincial' version of the Short Bros AEC-design body, with 50 seats and conventional fully-glazed cab with full-height door. In a fleet which already had standard Leyland-bodied Titans it must have looked the closely-related style it really was, particularly with the destination indicator also very like that standardised by Leyland, in use. The unladen weight of these early Regents was around 5 tons 13 cwt, a remarkably low figure by modern standards, even allowing for the modest 25ft. by 7ft. 6in. dimensions, comparing very favourably with a typical modern 11-metre single-decker with similar seating capacity.

Birmingham Corporation Tramways and Omnibus Department was the first operator to place a bulk order for Regents. However, the first two of the 30 vehicles with Brush bodywork mostly delivered towards the end of 1929 were chassis 661010 and 011 of the original dozen pre-production batch dating from July 1929, becoming Nos. 338-9, registered OF 3970 and 3971. In this picture showing fourteen of the batch, they can be identified as being respectively on the extreme left and fifth from the right, their early-type radiators being clearly visible. Other vehicles identifiable include No. 344 [second left], the first Birmingham straight-staircase bus, on chassis 661066.

Among the initial batch of vehicles completed by about July 1929, when this picture was taken, was this vehicle, painted in Glasgow Corporation livery, except for a non-standard silver roof, and bearing the name of the General Manager of that undertaking, Mr L. Mackinnon, but in fact a demonstrator. It differed from all the others in having a low-height [under 13ft.] body by Hall, Lewis & Co Ltd, to a design introduced by that firm, initially on a Dennis H chassis, the previous year. The style suited the Regent chassis particularly well, with its upper-deck front windows in a vee formation [a feature that was to be widely copied over the next few years] and shapely enclosed rear-end. Hall, Lewis' design had sunken gangways on each side of the upper-deck as shown in the cross-section on page 10, thus avoiding infringing the Leyland lowbridge body patents covering a single-gangway bus. AEC may have backed the wrong horse in sending this vehicle to Glasgow, however, as that undertaking was turning away from the lowbridge body, doubtless finding it inconvenient for city operation, and about to take delivery of what may have been the first 'Hybridge' [ie normal-height] version of the Leyland-bodied Titan, as shown on page 14 of 'Best of British Buses No 1'. It is now known that this vehicle, which another view shows as having the prototype style of radiator, was chassis number 661012, and became an AEC staff bus in June 1930.

By about November 1929, 661001, the original demonstrator registered MT 2114, had been freshly repainted in Glasgow livery. This may have been to allow evaluation of the Regent in normal-height form in that city. However, the livery as well as this particular bus had caught the imagination of Halifax Corporation, which had ordered its first three new Regents to a virtually identical specification, one being photographed apparently within a few days of this picture [negative number 0164] being taken by the AEC photographer. One wonders whether it had been the lowbridge demonstrator which had impressed the Halifax authorities with its livery style, since there would hardly have been time for the new Halifax buses to appear in the same style. Even so, this famous bus was soon sold to Halifax, being delivered on 17th February 1930 and remaining there as No. 57 until 1935.

Nottingham Corporation was another very early customer for a fleet of Regents, with two orders for ten chassis which were intermingled, all having bodywork by English Electric though fifteen were of conventional rear-entrance layout and five had centre entrances. No. 7, TV 721, on chassis 661029, one of the rear-entrance vehicles, is seen here when quite new — the batch were delivered before the end of 1929. The body style combined the AEC-inspired camel roof with styling very similar to that used for six English Electric six-wheel trolleybuses supplied to Nottingham at the same time, before English Electric linked up with AEC for the joint marketing of trolleybus chassis built by the latter. Though not unlike the LGOC's designs of the period in profile, the exaggerated bow front for the upper-deck gave them a rather ponderous appearance. The production version of the radiator, with its more harmonious curves at the top, was now standard.

Chapter Two:
1,000 Regents in the first year.

The new models were not announced publicly until the Autumn of 1929, but the original prototype demonstrator had begun to attract orders earlier in the year. AEC chassis numbers were generally allocated in sales order sequence and so it can be deduced that Birmingham was first in the queue for vehicles built after

Halifax Corporation's No. 53 [CP 8009] on chassis 661039, was one of three similar vehicles delivered in November 1929. On the original of this picture the Short Bros transfer can clearly be read on the staircase side, confirming AEC service records indicating this bodybuilder for 661038-40, which have also been attributed to Hoyal. The AEC negative numbers for the pictures of this vehicle, 0167 and 0168, suggest that they were taken very soon after that of MT 2114 opposite.

The five centre-entrance English Electric-bodied Nottingham Regents delivered towards the end of 1929 were very early examples of this layout as applied to double-deckers, possibly the first in Britain, pre-dating the Roe-bodied vehicle built for Grimsby Corporation by several months. They had a single staircase and could thus seat 26 upstairs and 24 down, only one less in total than the equivalent rear-entrance Nottingham buses. This view shows No. 18 [TV 738] on chassis 661056 as newly repainted in April 1935 in the revised livery in use by that date. It reveals the rather unsatisfactory contrast between the rounded front-end of the upper-deck and the square-cut canopy over the cab. English Electric were again to become associated with the centre-entrance layout slightly later particularly in regard to Blackpool trams.

the initial pre-production batch of a dozen. At first, ten were added to the two included in that dozen, but two further orders followed in quick succession and so 661010/1, 013-22, 045-54 and 065-72 were treated as a single batch of 30 in the Birmingham fleet (not 40 as the author erroneously stated in 'Blue Triangle').

Other early customers were also mainly municipal — Nottingham, Halifax and Newcastle, the total of vehicles delivered complete with bodywork by the end of 1929 being around 75 or so, though not all had entered service. Significantly, the first example for London General's own fleet was chassis number 661074, given the fleet number ST1 and registered UU 6614, and although first licensed in October 1929, it was not revealed to the press until January 1930, apparently because of some hesitation by the Public Carriage Office of the Metropolitan Police, responsible for licensing buses for service in London in those days. This was evidently because of its all-enclosed bodywork, built to a new design by LGOC in its Chiswick workshops. The first of the six-wheeled LS double-deckers of 1927 had originally had enclosed-stair bodywork but were soon converted to open staircase in response to such pressure and the prototype six-wheeled Renown model, chassis number 663001, completed for LGOC service and given the fleet number

The author's regard for AEC Regents dates back to the late 'thirties and journeys to and from school in examples in the fleet of Newcastle Corporation of which the vehicle shown when new, No. 99 [VK 1288] on chassis 661041, was the oldest. It was the first of four with normal-height Hall, Lewis 52-seat bodywork delivered towards the end of 1929 but placed in service in January 1930. These had open staircases, but four generally similar buses with closed stairs were delivered after the Hall, Lewis concern became Park Royal Coachworks Ltd later in 1930, together with six having English Electric bodies of a more conventional piano-fronted style than the Nottingham version. No. 99 was not infrequently used on a morning 'school special' journey around 1937-39 and the author can still recall descending that staircase on rainy mornings — oddly enough one did not get noticeably wet so long as the bus was still travelling reasonably fast, as these Regents tended to do on the stretch of the Great North Road heading into the city from the north. The polished front wheel-nut guard rings, an AEC innovation, added to the smart appearance.

A graphic indication of the impression created by the London General Omnibus Company's new fleet of lively and quiet-running AEC Regent buses when they began to enter service in the Spring of 1930 is given by this picture of ST55 at Marble Arch. Apart from the NS-type visible behind the horse on the left, all the older buses visible have solid tyres and three are open-toppers. The new ST fleet was more or less directly replacing the K-type buses of 1919-20, of which K364 is seen in the centre of the picture. ST55, on chassis number 661263, was new in March 1930, the LGOC-built 49-seat body having no windscreen to conform to the requirements of the Metropolitan Police's Public Carriage Office. Most of the LGOC ST buses did not have windscreens as built but they were eventually permitted by about April 1931 and the early vehicles rapidly converted. In other respects the ST specification was very up-to-date and the appearance achieved particularly harmonious, with nicely-judged blend of curves and straight lines. ST55 remained in service until July 1949, having spent part of the war period on loan to the Lincolnshire Road Car Co Ltd.

LT1 a couple of months earlier also had an open staircase, as did the following 149 production examples of this model supplied to LGOC in 1929-30.

The fleet number code ST applied to this and subsequent LGOC Regents indicated "Short T", the plain designation T being given to the slightly longer Regal single-decker model, while LT ("Long T") was used for the Renown six-wheeler which was marginally longer still. These were not particularly logical designations since the T was clearly not going to be the main type and a further complication became necessary later. The bodywork on ST1 was of an interesting design and there was a noteworthy degree of unanimity of thought on the general proportions of the bodywork between Birmingham Corporation and the LGOC, with only a short overhang of the passenger-carrying part of the upper-deck above the driver's cab and a rear-end profile which was completely upright from lower-deck waistrail to upper-deck roof. The first two Birmingham examples on chassis 661010 and 011, were evidently completed first but their designer may have seen LGOC drawings.

However, the LGOC design had what was then a novel internal feature, the straight staircase leading from a full-width platform and emerging almost half-way along the upper-deck. Slightly later, Birmingham incorporated a very similar design in one of its first 30 Regents, No. 344, subsequently adopting this feature as standard (and retaining it in only slightly modified form until the last rear-entrance buses built for Birmingham in the 'fifties), but LGOC appears to have been the originator. The LGOC design, though rather conservative in basic outline compared to the contemporary Leyland body, for example, was particularly harmonious in its detail execution, with subtleties such as the curvature of the projecting roof sections over both the cab and upper-deck which matched that of the top of the radiator. By comparison the initial Birmingham version, with harsher outlines and exaggerated piano-front effect, seemed rather heavy-handed, though later versions crept nearer to the ST style in detail design.

ST1 was passed for service early in 1930, with seating capacity reduced from the original 50 to 49 (in later years reduced again to 48) and with the glass windscreen removed — LGOC drivers had to do without windscreens at the behest of the Public Carriage Office until 1931. The first production batch of ST-type buses did not begin to come out of the LGOC Chiswick body shop until shortly before the end of February 1930, when 20 examples entered service.

Meanwhile, further batches for provincial operators were completed. Prominent among these were 661082-106 for Glasgow Corporation, an order which John Rackham may well have found encouraging, coming from the operator that had set the seal of success on the Titan, even though it was for only 25 chassis as compared to the 100 TD1 models order two years previously. In fact Glasgow did ultimately become a big Regent customer but not until the late 'thirties. City of Oxford Motor Services Ltd was to prove a more consistent user, as 661107-124 were to be the first of a long series of Oxford orders for Regents — indeed no other model of double-decker was added to that fleet during the period of this volume. The low-height bodywork on this first batch were by Hall, Lewis and they were of similar design

City of Oxford Motor Services Ltd was one of the most consistent Regent users, starting with a batch of eighteen with Hall, Lewis 48-seat low-height bodywork very like that on the early demonstrator painted in full Glasgow livery. No. 124 [WL 9043] on chassis 661108 is seen here when quite new. Oxford had been one of the limited number of provincial customers for NS-type buses and one is seen in the background. This early batch of Regents was one of few to be sold off before the outbreak of the 1939-45 war but although this vehicle went to a showman, several others remained in passenger service with independent operators, some being rebodied as coaches after the war.

to that on the early demonstrator, with sunken gangways on each side of the upper-deck, thus not infringing the Leyland patent. Short Bros also built a somewhat similar style of bodywork fitted to a number of early Regents including some supplied for operation by fleets associated with the LGOC (and operating in what was later to become the country area of London Transport, which ultimately took them over), including six fitted to chassis numbered in the first production batch of ST-type buses.

However, other country cousins of LGOC received Regents fitted with bodies to the LGOC ST design but in this case built by Ransomes, Sims and Jefferies. Some eighteen were ordered for Autocar Services Ltd and 42 for the East Surrey Traction Co Ltd and these, based on chassis with numbers between 661143 and 209, entered service early in 1930. Most of them ultimately received ST numbers, but not until 1935. During this period, AEC chassis numbers became more intermingled than usual, and also within this range were vehicles for such operators as Newcastle Corporation and the Devon-based Southern General fleet, as well as the second 'true' ST chassis, 661148 which, although allocated the fleet number ST2, was allocated to LGOC's training fleet fitted with an old open-top body from a K-type bus of the early 'twenties when received in November 1929 and not fitted with a new body until May 1931, when it was registered GO 7156.

The first production batch of ST-type buses for LGOC was 661211-509 which, with one exception, became ST3-301 in sequence, mostly with various batches of GC, GF and GH registration numbers, generally issued when the buses were completed and hence not in order; most were delivered by the late summer of 1930. The majority had LGOC-built 49-seat bodies to largely similar design to ST1, though with a rounded shape of cab front, also differing in

this respect from the Ransomes version. A further batch of chassis for LGOC were 661783-999, which became ST502-517, 154 (replacing the chassis originally allocated which had been diverted to Chariot, a London independent operator) and 302-501. These again had LGOC-pattern 49-seat bodies, though some were built by Short Bros or Strachans rather than at Chiswick. Most were in service by the end of 1930.

The gap between the two 1930 LGOC batches, 661510-782, was filled by vehicles for other operators. Repeat orders were already coming in — notably another 20 for Nottingham, a further 75 for Birmingham and further vehicles for Chester, Newcastle and National (or more specifically Eastern and Southern National). However, a major new customer was Thomas Tilling Ltd which now followed up the short-lived use of 661004 with an order for 136 chassis, 661553-688, with fleet numbers beginning at 6001, though not in sequence, for operation on services in Brighton (the first twelve fleet numbers) or, for the remaining 124, London. The Tilling company had hitherto generally fulfilled its vehicle needs from Tilling-Stevens, which was until 1930 an associated company, but this connection was in the process of being broken. There had been a measure of agreement between Tilling and the LGOC for many years and as the Regent had been found a suitable vehicle the change was logical, though no doubt surprising to onlookers at the time. However, Tilling maintained its own rather conservative ideas on bodywork, so these vehicles had open-staircase bodywork of Tilling's distinctive, if rather dated design, built either by Tilling itself or Dodson. The batch were placed in service during the Summer and Autumn of 1930.

On the formation of London Transport in 1933, the London-based buses were added to the ST class, receiving what were then the next

vacant numbers ST 837 upwards.

With about a thousand chassis in service or at bodybuilders in the year since the model was announced, the Regent had certainly made its mark by the Autumn of 1930, even if more than half of this total were in London. The production rate was evidently slightly faster than Leyland achieved with the TD1 of which 773 chassis were built from September 1929 to September 1930. There had been only minor changes mechanically and most of the vehicles had the original size of 100 mm bore 6.1-litre engine, which could give a surprisingly lively performance in the hands of an enterprising driver. A larger 110 mm bore unit, having a swept volume of 7.4-litres, had been provided for within the initial design, and a few vehicles with this engine had been built — one of the first to be ordered, in October 1929, was 661081 for Australia. Among experimental variations, perhaps the most remarkable was the experimental eight-cylinder engine fitted to two of the LGOC buses ST4 (661212) and ST84 (661292) when new early in 1930 — it was of smaller bore to give about the same swept volume as the 100 mm unit, and should, on paper, have been impressively smooth. However, the standard six was so good in this respect that it is difficult to imagine that much could have been gained for so elaborate a redesign — evidently this was the conclusion reached at the time, as standard engines were fitted by the end of the year.

Body design was passing through a fascinating transitional stage. The original AEC-design open-staircase camel-roof body had only a limited following after the initial batch of prototypes. Halifax Corporation continued to specify it until 1931, later examples being built by Hoyal, a concern which built both car and bus bodies and was soon to become a victim of the depression years. A handful went to other fleets, notably

Glasgow Corporation took delivery of 25 Regents early in 1930. They had locally-built normal-height Cowieson bodywork, to a design which had by then been chosen as standard for the Leyland Titan TD1 which were to remain in the majority for Glasgow orders until 1931. No. 255 [GE 7287] on chassis 661086, is seen when new, followed by a 1922 Humber 15.9 hp tourer.

[Right] Short Bros introduced a revised body style derived from the AEC design early in 1930 in both normal-height and low-height versions, somewhat reminiscent of the Hall, Lewis 1929-30 style, but with a more rounded rear-end. This vehicle, number 29 in the Amersham & District fleet on chassis 661133, was new in April 1930, having a 48-seat lowbridge body. It was taken over by London Transport in November 1933, becoming ST1089 and was to be one of the longest-lived of the class, surviving until February 1952, latterly with oil engine.

the Cornish Bus/Southern General concern.

However, Hall, Lewis had developed a rather attractive style with upper-deck windscreen set in a slight vee-formation, first seen on a Dennis H chassis in 1928. It was originally a low-height design, with upper-deck seats arranged in herringbone formation and sunken gangways on both sides. A few examples had been built on TD1 chassis, but it suited the Regent particularly well, the 1930 Oxford vehicles being perhaps the best-known, though a normal-height version was also built for Newcastle (including some with open stairs) and Southampton. Later examples were built after the Hall, Lewis business was taken over by Park Royal. It may have been this that led to a revised version of the camel-roof body, with rather similar front-end

and enclosed stairs with a single comparatively small rear window in each deck and well-rounded contours. Examples were built by Short Bros for several operators and also by Park Royal for Nottingham.

However, the camel-roof never really caught on in a big way, and Short Bros evolved a distinctive style of its own, again with the vee-formation upper-deck windscreen, but having a more sloping profile. Though not exclusive to Regent chassis, it was one of the most familiar types of body on this model in the 1930-32 period and evidently met with AEC approval, several being used as demonstrators.

The LGOC design of body also had its following even outside that operating group, two examples being built by Ransomes for the West Bridgford fleet and in 1931 six for the

Exeter municipal fleet, while a demonstrator built for Leicester and a vehicle lent to Sweden (which in those days drove on the left of the road) were also produced. No doubt part of the appeal was the glamour of having a replica of a London bus and, to the author at least, there was an undeniable air of dignity about such vehicles.

Other London operators, both Tilling and independent, seemed to be caught up in a curious situation where they were fitting bodywork of styles reminiscent of the 'twenties to the most modern-looking chassis, doubtless mainly because of the conservatism of the Metropolitan Police. In general, however, the trend was to sleeker and more modern styles and Regent chassis were often to be the basis of advanced styles of bodywork as indicated in later chapters.

[Above] The revised Short Bros body was available in camel-roof form, as represented by No. 122 in the Southern General Omnibus Co Ltd fleet, seen leaving Plymouth for Plympton soon after delivery early in 1930. Registered DR 6741 and based on chassis 661141, this vehicle passed to the Western National Omnibus Co Ltd as number 3271 in 1931, being converted to diesel in 1935 with a Gardner 6LW engine and rebodied by Beadle in 1945, not being withdrawn until 1955. Note the Plymouth Corporation open-top tram on the left of the picture and the contemporary feminine fashions. The advertisement on the wall behind the bus refers to tours by Southern General's Blue Line coaches.

[Below left] Less well-known was the Hall, Lewis/Park Royal version of the camel-roof AEC specification body in its 1930 form. It had an even more extreme hump effect, as conveyed by this high-angle picture of Nottingham Corporation No. 32 [TV 1632] on chassis 661528. [Below right] Nottingham's 1930 batch was equally divided between Park Royal and Short Bros and this picture, dating from 1935, like that on the left, shows the front-end of No. 27 [on chassis 661522] and the rear of No. 30, both with Short Bros body. The rear view conveys the characteristic rear-end, with single relatively narrow windows with generously radiused corners in both upper and lower decks — there is evidence of AEC and, in all probability, personal Rackham influence here [compare with AEC Q designs shown on pages 10 and to a lesser extent 95 of 'Best of British Buses No. 2'].

However, when viewed from any distance, the camel-roof body design took on a faintly comical appearance and it was not long before the more attractive effect of an elliptical cross-section became almost universally preferred. Short Bros adopted a well-rounded style which suited the Regent chassis and was the natural successor to the AEC design, although also built on other makes of chassis. Here Cumberland Motor Services Ltd No. 12 [RM 7328], chassis 661781, a single vehicle delivered later in 1930, threads its way through the back streets of Whitehaven. It was sold to Seamark of Rushden and then in January 1937 was taken over with part of that concern's business by the United Counties Omnibus Co Ltd, becoming that operator's No. 441.

A similar but slightly earlier vehicle, one of three supplied to Colchester Corporation, is seen in the summer of 1930 at the railway station soon after entering service, the intending passengers in the foreground having doubtless just arrived on a train from London. The garage in the background indicates the growth of motoring — the car wash facility, unusual at the time, was relatively expensive, as 2s. 6d. [12½p] would have bought two gallons of petrol. Note the LNER [ex-Great Eastern] locomotives in the right background.

Thomas Tilling Ltd, though growing closer to the LGOC as indicated by its choice of the Regent after standardising on Tilling-Stevens buses since before the 1914-18 war, still had its own decidedly conservative ideas on bus design. Hence the bodywork on the fleet of 136 Regents placed in service in 1930 — and indeed further batches added to the London and Brighton-based fleets up to 1932 — were to an open-staircase style which seemed to belong more to the 'twenties than the 'thirties. The chassis incorporated a number of non-standard features, such as the direct attachment of the dash and cab structure to the frame [an idea going out of favour at the time though still used by some other makers]. On the other hand the front mudguards were somewhat similar to AEC's later standard as adopted from 1932. Some of the bodies were built in Tilling's own bodybuilding works and some to the same Tilling design by Dodson, a concern which catered largely for operators in London. The vehicles were numbered 6001 upwards, the first 100 having registrations which ran in corresponding sequence from GJ 2001 upwards, though the chassis numbers were not in precise order. The first dozen buses were allocated to Brighton, so 6017 seen here at Marble Arch soon after delivery in June 1930 was one the first few in London, its chassis number being 661568. When London Transport was formed, this vehicle became ST841 and was one of a small proportion of these buses withdrawn immediately after the outbreak of war, although it saw further service as a staff bus with the British Broadcasting Corporation.

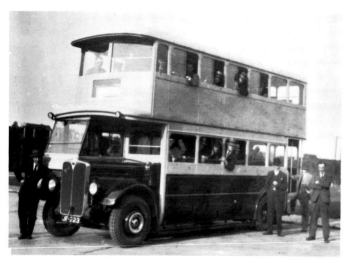

[Above] Some provincial municipalities were attracted by the LGOC body design and a demonstrator to Leicester Corporation was bodied by Ransomes to this style, though having full-drop lower-deck windows and sliding windows upstairs. It also had an early example of the 110 mm-bore 7.4-litre petrol engine, publicised at the time as the 110 hp six-cylinder. Registered JF 223, it was not purchased by Leicester, being sold to G. F. Campion & Co of Ruddington and, being slightly lower than most provincial centre-gangway double-deckers, was able to operate under a bridge which caused other operators to buy lowbridge buses. It passed to Barton Transport in 1936. It is seen here at Southall when new. The chassis number was 661129.

[Below] Provincial orders for Regents of the LGOC ST style were bodied by Ransomes, Sims & Jefferies Ltd of Ipswich, the resulting vehicles being very like the 60 examples built there for the East Surrey and Autocar fleets in the Spring of 1930 and resembling ST1 in having the square-fronted cab with windscreen. Two vehicles for West Bridgford Urban District Council were built at the same time, and No. 19 [VO 3878] on chassis 661768 is seen at Southall before delivery. West Bridgford, just outside Nottingham, was one of the few UDC bus fleets, and kept its vehicles to an exceptionally high standard. This photograph conveys the classic lines of the ST particularly well.

[Below] The General Manager of Grimsby Corporation and Mr Charles H. Roe of the bodybuilding concern of that name co-operated in developing and patenting a new design of centre-entrance double-staircase double-decker, the first example being built on Regent chassis 661777 and delivered to the Grimsby fleet as No. 38, registered EE 9860, on 2nd August 1930. It was also the first Roe-bodied Regent, a combination that was to become more familiar in the later 'thirties when Leeds standardised on such vehicles, though with rear entrances. Grimsby, and in 1931-2 Burnley, took further centre-entrance Regents of later styles, however, supply of the former continuing until 1937. Unfortunately, this prototype body was destroyed by bombing during the war but the chassis went back to Roe and re-emerged in December 1943 with a 'utility' rear-entrance body. Note the revised bonnet louvre layout introduced at this period.

WEST BRIDGFORD URBAN DISTRICT COUNCIL

19

Several London independent operators were willing to buy Regent chassis built by a concern which was an offshoot of their great rival, the LGOC. Four bought individual 15ft. 6½ in.-wheelbase chassis, all with characteristically conservative styles of open-staircase bodywork, and these became ST1028-1031, when taken over by London Transport. Edward Gilchrist Hope, the proprietor of the Pembroke fleet, placed GJ 3020, on chassis 661777, in service in May 1930, and this became ST1031 when acquired by LT. The bodywork, built by Birch Bros, then also an independent bus operator in London, though not an AEC customer, was very like that on a Regent supplied to Chariot at about the same time [later ST1028]. Surprisingly, both seated 56, [30 upstairs, 26 down] an unusually high total for the time, when new, though subsequently reduced to 52 and 54 seats at different times with LT. GJ 3020 was in store at Bull Yard, Peckham, when it was destroyed in an air raid in October 1940.

[Below, left] Operators outside central London were not subject to the Public Carriage Office and hence Amersham and District's second Regent, placed in service the same month as the vehicle shown above on chassis 661775, looked much more up-to-date. No. 30 [KX 5055], seen at Windsor Castle, had a Strachans 48-seat low-height body clearly influenced by AEC styling ideas of the time, though with echoes of Manchester's fleet of Leyland TD1 buses, of which Strachans had just bodied a dozen, at the rear of the upper-deck. It became ST1090, surviving in service until September 1951.

[Below] The other two central-area ex-independent ST-type buses had Dodson 54-seat bodywork, both dating from September 1930. This one, VX 7553, was owned by a concern with the title Pro Bono Publico Ltd, becoming ST1030. It became another Bull Yard casualty in 1940.

Briefly, during 1931, the Regent was chosen for a major part of the intake of new buses for Walsall Corporation, a total of fourteen entering service, together with thirteen Dennis Lance. Seven of the Regents which entered service early in the year had Short Bros bodywork of a design derived from the 1930 style but with a new more sloping front-end, with convex rather than concave shaping of the upper-deck waistrail under the front windows. This was Short Bros latest standard, modernising a design which was already one of the most up-to-date in a rapidly developing era. Walsall also specified five-bay construction rather than the six-bay layout usual in this basic design and straight staircase layout, the resulting seating capacity being 26 upstairs and 22 down. The chassis had the 110 mm bore 7.4-litre petrol-engine, by then officially standard, though the 100 mm unit continued to be favoured by the two largest Regent customers, the LGOC and Thomas Tilling. No. 40 [DH 8513] was on chassis 6611099 and, with the rest of the batch, was withdrawn in 1944.

Chapter Three: Broadening the appeal.

The mechanical specification of the large numbers of Regents sold in 1929-31 largely followed the pattern of the Titan TD1 in being remarkably standardised, except in relatively trivial items such as choice of auxiliary engine equipment, despite the much greater variety of bodywork. The standard vehicle was well able to attract orders from operators of widely differing character.

However, a major change was on the way, with several revisions of the standard design and important new options. Clearly, Rackham believed in remaining one jump

ahead of the opposition, even though plenty of business was still coming in, and moreover was able to persuade AEC's management of the wisdom of such a policy.

The majority of vehicles built continued to have the 6-type petrol engine and conventional gearbox, at any rate until about 1933, but both units were revised. The proportion of customers specifying the 110 mm-bore engine increased significantly from 1931, though LGOC still favoured the 100 mm bore size for the ST. A further stage of development occurred in 1932 with the introduction

of the so-called 'high-power head' A162 version of the 110 mm 7.4-litre engine. This was the final stage of petrol engine development for the Regent and its output of 120 bhp was for some years the highest standardised in a British petrol bus chassis in regular production.

The gearbox, hitherto with sliding engagement for all indirect gears, now acquired a constant-mesh third speed which made changes into this ratio easier, but didn't alter the characteristic Regent sound as the gear teeth themselves remained of the same form — sales literature

The wind of change away from a single basically standard chassis began to blow in December 1930, when AEC introduced its first production oil engine, the 8.1-litre A155 unit. This picture shows members of the Municipal Tramways and Transport Association at the special oil engine Show held at Southall that month. They were posed in front of a petrol-engined Regent with Short Bros body and, on the right, ST464, chassis number 661962, one of three LGOC buses briefly fitted with the new engine and instantly identifiable as such by the projecting radiator required to accommodate the A155's greater length as compared to the standard unit. Another photograph taken on the same occasion shows that the petrol-engined bus was not then registered, but its appearance and livery appear identical to those of 661782, registered JA 1291 at about that date for demonstration to Stockport Corporation, though not purchased by that undertaking and subsequently acquired by the Midland General concern.

reference to a 'silent third' was no more than wishful thinking.

This change was mainly intended to improve ease of driving in city operation, almost certainly as a result of LGOC influence, and the same doubtless applied to the steering which changed from the original Marles type to an AEC-manufactured worm-and-nut design. The latter was noticeably lower geared and much lighter. Similar units were used on almost all subsequent AEC passenger chassis, making them much less of a trial of strength than most full-sized bus chassis, until the advent of power-assistance, yet retaining a very precise feel. It was probably the six-wheeled Renown that was largely in mind, for LGOC had decided to place large numbers of this model in service in 1931-32 forming the bulk of the LT class and such vehicles were inherently less nimble than the ST, though the latter were also converted to worm-and-nut steering.

Another change to the standard Regent specification was an increase of wheelbase from 15ft. 6½in. to 16ft. 3in. This was a consequence of an increase in the permitted overall length from 25ft. to 26ft. The first examples were built in time for the November 1931 Olympia Show and were fitted with lightweight bodywork capable of seating 60 passengers. For a time both lengths were built simultaneously but the 16ft. 3in. version had become usual by about a year later. The LGOC produced its own design of 60-seat bodywork and introduced a new type designation, STL, literally signifying 'Short T Long', to indicate this version, entering service at the beginning of 1933. These swung future London bus orders back to the Regent as its highest seating-capacity Renowns accommodated no more passengers.

Historically, it is interesting to note that Thomas Tilling Ltd, co-operating even more closely with LGOC in its bus policy for London operation, allocated LGOC-style numbers to a batch of 16ft. 3in. Regents. The first one was originally numbered ST837, indicating that it had not at that stage been decided to begin a fresh number series for the longer type of Regent, but this was almost immediately changed to STL51, thus following the first 50 of the later type in LGOC's own fleet. Only a few months later, both LGOC and Tilling's London operations had been brought into the newly-formed London Passenger Transport Board's empire, and the earlier Tilling Regents received ST-series numbers, the first one becoming ST837, the number originally allocated to STL51.

However, to return to vehicle specifications, the most significant news was the introduction of alternative engine and transmission options. AEC had produced an experimental oil (diesel) engine as early as 1928 and this was used in a works six-wheeled bus of the same 802-type as the LGOC's LS-type pioneer six-wheelers by December of that year. Useful experience was gained, but a quite different design of engine was produced by C. B. Dicksee, who had been appointed by Rackham for this task and was soon to become recognised as one of the most eminent pioneers of British oil engine development. This was the A155 engine, a six-cylinder 8.1-litre unit having a certain visual similarity to the 6-type petrol engine, due to similar exhaust manifolds and other details but was in fact quite different internally, with push-rod operated valves, quite apart from the Acro-type combustion chambers and fuel injection equipment associated with the

different fuel.

It was announced in October 1930 and by December of that year, several Regents including three LGOC ST-type buses had been fitted with this engine, and others followed in the Spring of 1931, being delivered to operators in various parts of the country. Despite being more heavily built than the petrol unit, they were not entirely trouble-free. Fred Sloan has told me something of the troubles he met as an experimental department fitter, based at the Birmingham AEC depot. Apparently the timing had to be exactly right or there was a danger of a collision between piston and a valve. Another weakness stemmed from the lack of a top-speed governor on these early units.

An oil engine of this early type in a Walsall Corporation Regent had suffered damage due to a broken timing chain and a replacement was being taken to it from Southall in an AEC Majestic demonstration lorry with the same type of engine when the latter 'blew up', due to over-enthusiastic driving. With no governor, these engines would run at very high speeds but the high stresses had not been fully appreciated, and subsequently governors were fitted. So the replacement engine was fitted to the Majestic and the Walsall engine repaired by working day and night to enable that vehicle to be put back in service.

However, work was soon put in hand on revised designs and in 1932, a much improved engine had appeared. This was the 8.8-litre A165 unit, using a new type of combustion chamber developed by the Ricardo concern of consulting engineers. Although derived from the A155, it had been strengthened, becoming a reliable unit as well as considerably more powerful, developing some 130

Several operators, mainly municipalities, placed individual oil-engined Regents with the newly-introduced AEC-Acro 8.1-litre engine in service during 1931. Some had the standard six-bay Short Bros body that was in effect the contemporary AEC standard, but some operators chose versions of their own standard designs. Thus 6611156, supplied to City of Leicester Tramways and Motor Omnibus Department, had Brush bodywork of the sloping piano-front style then favoured by this bodybuilder and supplied to quite a number of municipalities. This style was also Leicester's contemporary standard, normally on Leyland Titan chassis. However, it was noteworthy that it had a straight staircase, with seating for 28 passengers upstairs and 20 down, probably inspired by the petrol Regent demonstrator with ST-style body briefly operated the previous year. No. 53 was part of the permanent fleet, however, and remained in service until 1947, considerably longer than most of these vehicles, which were still largely experimental. Leicester was later to become a regular customer for oil-engined AEC double-deckers, but not until 1937.

bhp and thus giving greater performance potential than even the new A162 petrol engine. It was, however, a heavier and longer engine than the 6-type petrol units and although the LGOC began to take sizeable numbers in 1932, they were in LT-type Renown six-wheelers in which there was no problem with dimensions.

Most of the early 8.8 Regents went to municipal fleets but the numbers involved were at first fairly small, choice of this option gaining more momentum in 1933-34.

Meanwhile another important development was the offering of a fluid coupling and preselective epicyclic gearbox as an option to the conventional clutch and gearbox. The preselective gearbox had been developed by Walter Gordon Wilson but it was Daimler that had effected the happy marriage of this unit with the fluid coupling, which was christened the 'fluid flywheel'. In view of the relatively recent break-up of Associated Daimler, it was significant that Lord Ashfield, who was again personally involved, thought it sensible to arrange with Daimler an agreement which gave AEC the right to use the fluid flywheel and preselective gearbox. In the early days, complete units were supplied by Daimler, and although quite a number of private car makers used preselective gearboxes of the same Wilson type, AEC was the only concern outside the Daimler empire to offer the complete Daimler transmission as a production option.

LGOC's original trials had involved the purchase of three Daimler CH6 double-deckers, numbered DST1-3, and early applications to AEC chassis for LGOC involved Renown 663-type six-wheeler models of the LT class which formed the bulk of deliveries in 1931-32, though it had originally been intended that two ST-type buses would also be involved, ST746 and 747. So the first example in a Regent for the LGOC fleet did not enter service until early 1933 when the last of the first batch of STL buses, STL50, on chassis number 6612120 appeared so equipped. So the earliest fluid transmission Regents went elsewhere, ironically among the first being 6611810, placed in service by a London independent operator, E. Brickwood Ltd (Redline) in May 1932, which was also a very early 16ft. 3in. wheelbase Regent (later becoming STL558), and 6611862-7 for the Oxford fleet. The latter were delivered in July-August 1932, where they were received with such lack of enthusiasm by the management that no further fluid transmission Regents were ever supplied to this operator. The BET group, to which Oxford belonged, remained hesitant about fluid transmission throughout most of its period of involvement with buses.

However, municipal users were more attracted to the concept and Huddersfield, Leeds and Newcastle Corporations all took early examples at about the same time, all subsequently standardising on fluid transmission buses. Admittedly Newcastle, which had split its orders between AEC and Daimler from 1930, chose Daimler chassis for almost all

its needs in the later 'thirties, but Regents with fluid transmission were to remain standard in the Leeds and Huddersfield fleets until the 'fifties.

Another option introduced at the same time was Lockheed hydraulic operation of the brakes. The vacuum servo was retained but the hydraulic system eliminated the need for the somewhat complex so-called triple-servo system which had been introduced to improve braking performance about a year earlier, and after a year or so vacuum-hydraulic operation of the brakes became standard on AEC passenger chassis, remaining so until the wartime era.

Another development introduced during this era of rapid change was the fully-floating rear axle, in which the half-shafts were relieved of all stress due to the weight of the vehicle. This required a larger hub and was introduced in production Regents during 1933, though there may have been isolated earlier examples and it was also possible to convert earlier vehicles, though this was rarely done.

Despite this spate of new features, most of the Regents built in 1931 were substantially similar to those produced in 1930, except that on 'provincial' examples (ie those for operators outside London) more had the 110 mm bore engine. Beginning at 6611000, the chassis number batches consisted at first of mainly provincial buses, though including 62 for Tilling's London fleet 6611028-89 (subsequently numbered ST961-

The third and last big batch of ST-type chassis for LGOC consisted of 319 buses [in reality orders for 300, 15 and 4] given the chassis numbers 6611163-1481 and having the fleet numbers ST518-817, 822-836 and 818-821, in that order. Most had Chiswick-built bodywork including the example shown, 6611413, registered GO 660, which entered service in April 1931 and was among the first of the production batch to be built with glass windscreens, though earlier vehicles were soon converted. Another feature to have changed from the original style was the single-panel lower-saloon rear window, in place of the previous divided type. This was associated with an increase in the cutaway of the rear panel at the kerb-side corner of the platform, designed to allow space for escape should the vehicle turn over on to its near side, as required by new regulations. Again, earlier ST buses were subsequently rebuilt to the revised design. This was rarely done on provincial buses; the regulations were not applied retrospectively. ST768 remained in service until May 1948, a fairly typical life-span for these vehicles.

Tilling also continued to take delivery of more Regents, with its standard open-staircase design of bodywork, which was even more out of step with contemporary trends by 1931-32. Identical buses were used in London and Brighton, and this scene in Brighton shows No. 6010 [GJ 2010] of the first batch of vehicles supplied in the Spring of 1930, with chassis number 661562, overtaking 6208 [GN 6208] built towards the end of the following year on chassis 6611522. The latter vehicle belonged to a batch which was exclusively operated in Brighton, but like all the Tilling-owned Regents, it was registered in London. The vehicles based in Brighton continued under Tilling ownership until 1935, when the Brighton Hove & District Omnibus Co Ltd was set up to take over this business. Both the buses shown were later re-engined and rebodied.

1022, though not in order). The last major batch of ST buses for LGOC were 6611163-1481, with numbers between ST518 and 836, mostly placed in service during the earlier part of 1931. From then until 6612070, deliveries were much more mixed, though there were further batches of ST-style buses for East Surrey and of open-staircase buses for Tilling,

mainly for operation in Brighton. Birmingham's last major delivery was a fleet of 60 delivered in 1931-32 (6611591-1650), which included 20 with Metro-Cammell metal-framed bodies. This followed good results with a 1930 bus, No. 209 (chassis 661766) which had the prototype body of this type, setting the pattern for later standard policy in Birmingham,

though this was another operator to switch to Daimler chassis after a brief spell of favour for the Birmingham-made Morris-Commercial until 1933.

As usual, chassis were by no means delivered in numerical order, but numbers after about 6611730 or so mostly entered service in 1932 and the switch to 1933 registrations

Both Great Yarmouth and Lowestoft Corporations placed batches of Regents in service in 1931, the bodywork contracts going to the United Automobile Services Ltd works at Lowestoft, which was on the point of being handed over [with that Company's bus services and vehicles operating in East Anglia] to the newly formed Eastern Counties Omnibus Co Ltd. The vehicle shown was the first of Great Yarmouth's five vehicles, No. 27 [EX 2874] and its chassis number, 6611543, suggests that this particular chassis may have been 'borrowed' from the Lowestoft order for eight, for the remainder of 6611541-8 were Lowestoft buses while the first vehicle of 661560-4 was a Lowestoft bus and the other four went to Great Yarmouth. The body design was of the piano-front style but incorporated a straight staircase. The photograph, though rather self-consciously posed, conveys something of the atmosphere of the fishwharf — one wonders what the fisher-girls were saying to the photographer!

coming about 400 chassis numbers later. Output of Regents had thus dropped in 1931-32 from that of the first twelve months, largely due to LGOC's emphasis on Renowns for its new bus needs during this period. However, AEC had picked up several important new customers as well as laying a good foundation for the future with its technical developments. The pattern of municipalities and major companies, largely those associated with BET, as the major customers for Regents outside London was becoming established.

Considerable effort went into this search for new customers in a period of general recession and intense competition. Fred Sloan told me how at Morecambe Corporation the choice of vehicle depended on comparative trials of AEC Regent, Daimler, Dennis Lance and Leyland Titan buses, with particular emphasis on petrol consumption. He managed to discover that though the Leyland wasn't doing quite so well as the AEC, the Dennis was giving a slightly better figure, while the Daimler had the advantage of being driven by a man who knew the district. The key to success was the climb of Heysham Hill and by setting the clutch stop 'tight', Fred managed a quick change up from second to third and improved the Regent's figures. AEC got the order, for six Regents and a Regal 4, and Morecambe, though not a large operator, was to remain a Regent stronghold for almost the whole of its separate existence as a bus operator. Other important orders

were received during this period from South Wales Transport Co Ltd, for a total of 50 Regents and Mansfield District Traction Co Ltd, where 34 Regents replaced a previous tram fleet.

The last order for 15ft. 6½in. chassis to be placed by an LGOC associate company was for London General Country Services Ltd, which was the new title of the former East Surrey Traction Co Ltd. It consisted of 23 chassis, 6612021-43, which were fitted with a new type of LGOC-built body similar in appearance to that on the 1932-type Renown six-wheelers generally called 'Bluebirds' after the colour of their upholstery, with upper-deck extended forward over the cab, although the seating capacity was for some reason restricted to 48. They were ready for service in August 1932, though some were stored until March 1933. They were not numbered at first but eventually became ST1070-79, 1032-9, and 1080-84.

Meanwhile the LGOC's first 16ft. 3in. Regents, 6612071-2120, with similar-looking but longer 60-seat bodies were entering service as STL1-50 from the beginning of 1933 and some of Tilling's slightly later batch of chassis numbers, 6612164-2243, were also on the road as STL51 upwards though the fleet numbers were not in order in this case.

Body design was in a period of rapid development during this period. The original camel-roof AEC-design body died out, being succeeded

largely by a vee-screen version by Short Bros. Park Royal and Brush also built similar styles for some operators and Roe became another recruit from 1932.

Meanwhile, however, Rackham had started off another chain of development with the new AEC-design body introduced with the first handful of 16ft. 3in. wheelbase chassis at the time of the 1931 Olympia Show. This had a continuous slope from the driver's windscreen to the upper-deck roof and a somewhat bulbous shape to the cab front (the latter probably inspired by the 1930-31 LGOC style). The front of the upper-deck was fairly rounded in plan, with windows set in a vee formation approximately to this outline. Park Royal and Brush built the first examples, and Park Royal produced a rather more upright version which became its standard during 1932. Weymann also built to a somewhat similar design, securing the above-mentioned initial Morecambe order and the bulk of that for Mansfield District.

Some operators continued to take an independent line, notably the LGOC, which continued the characteristic ST style and then jumped to the vertical-fronted 'Bluebird' style for the last few country examples and the first STL buses, and Tilling, which continued its open-stair body style until adopting quite a modern enclosed-stair outline for its version of the STL.

The Tynemouth & District Electric Traction Company had been part of the BET group since 1899 and operated electric trams between North Shields, Tynemouth and Whitley Bay from 1901 until August 1931. A demonstration AEC Regent with standard Short Bros 50-seat body, 661774, had been registered by the Northern General Transport Co Ltd, by then the 'parent' company, as CN 4520, for use by Tynemouth and although not retained [it passed to Borough Services Ltd of Southend], similar buses were decided upon for the tram replacement fleet. The first batch of six vehicles were registered in July 1931 and 6611586 is seen here soon after entry into service in Whitley Bay, with appropriate lettering to leave former tram passengers in no doubt. A further ten similar buses but with revised emergency exits were placed in service the following year, and from then until 1946, the NGT became a major AEC customer.

[Below] Birmingham Corporation placed another big fleet of 60 new Regents in service in 1931-32, bringing the total of this model in service to 167, all placed in service in a period of under three years. But they were to prove the last to be purchased, apart from five in 1937 and fifteen of the early post-war RT type in 1947. This cessation of business must have come as quite a blow to AEC when it became apparent with the placing of the orders for 1933, as there were also well over 200 older AEC double-deckers dating from the mid to late 'twenties in the current Birmingham fleet. There is clear evidence of several attempts to re-establish AEC sales to Birmingham, unsuccessful against an understandable wish to support local industry and the efficiency of the Gardner engine. The last 20 Regents played their part in this, having Birmingham-built Metro-Cammell bodies to Birmingham design, which had grown rather closer to LGOC's style in its appearance, as shown by No. 492 [OV 4492] on chassis 6611642.

[Above] Park Royal's body designs tended to vary, but this style built for Nottingham Corporation is typical of the 1931 standard style, apart from the route number position specified by the operator. No. 102 [TV 4493] on chassis 6611569, seen when newly in service, was one of a batch of five, but Nottingham took delivery of 30 generally similar-looking buses that year, of which 20 were bodied by Park Royal and ten by Brush. Some had six-bay bodywork but the chassis were basically standard 15ft. 6½ in. wheelbase models, Nottingham choosing to retain the 100 mm-bore engine. Of these, eleven, including No. 102 were operated by Venture Ltd Basingstoke after sale in 1944. Note the 1929 camel-roof English Electric-bodied Regent in the background.

[Below] When standard maximum dimensions for buses were fixed as a consequence of the 1930 Road Traffic Act, plans were made early in 1931 for the introduction of a 16ft. 3in. wheelbase Regent to suit the resulting 26ft. length. Among the first examples was chassis 6611158, apparently ordered as a demonstrator for Sheffield in February 1931 and delivered, numbered 66 and registered MV 105, in August of that year. Weymann, then virtually unknown as a builder of double-deck bodies, produced this rather ungainly lowbridge design, seating 22 mainly in rows of three on the double-gangway upper-deck and 26 downstairs. Emergency exits, then still a matter for experiment, were provided on the offside near the front on both decks. It ran briefly in London in 1940, when provincial buses were borrowed to augment the war-stricken LT fleet, and remained in service until 1946.

Another of the first demonstrator 16ft. 3in. wheelbase chassis, 6611159, was completed in the summer of 1931 with a new design of body that was clearly intended to set off a fresh line of development and make the latest Regent at least as much of an eye-catcher as had been the original 1929 design. Rackham had not lost interest in the appearance of complete vehicles and this was a fresh venture in the AEC-design body system. Built by Park Royal, it seated 56 [by early 1932 increased to 60, with 34 on top] in a fully-enclosed body with unladen weight held down to 5 tons 14 cwt, practically as low as the original open-stair 50-seat design. This was necessary if the laden weight was to be kept below 10 tons, the maximum then permissible. However, it is in the stylish outline that this design was far ahead of its time. The vehicle shown above was registered TV 4867 and briefly operated by Nottingham Corporation as No. 107 and then allocated the temporary number 107A before doing further demonstration work, eventually being sold to White [Imperial] of Cardiff and in 1936 becoming Western Welsh No. 579.

The almost identical looking body shown below was built to the same basic design by Brush, apparently for the November 1931 Olympia Show. The contours of the rear dome gave a subtle hint of later Brush standard designs and other differences included the radiused window corners [another feature well ahead of its time] and smooth external roof line. It is believed to have been based on chassis number 6611850, which was an identical-looking vehicle registered MV 842, by 1933 operating for Westcliff-on-Sea Motor Services Ltd in which fleet it was to remain.

Another of the 1931 Show chassis, 6611851, was fitted with a quite different design of body by Brush, becoming Walsall Corporation No. 1 [DH 9041]. All the 1931 Show Regents, 6611850-3, were built to the latest 16ft. 3in. wheelbase specification, nominally model 661/4, with the 120 bhp A162 petrol engine, constant-mesh gearbox and worm-and-nut steering. They also had new-style front mudguards in aluminium and polished rear wheel nut retaining rings, a feature sometimes found on Regals of this period but rarely, if ever, on other Regents. The longer wheelbase enabled the lower deck of Walsall No. 1 to seat 26, but the upper-deck capacity was 28 and the styling, with exaggerated vee-front upper-deck windows, was basically similar to that of a couple of Brush-bodied Regents supplied to Walsall earlier in the year. A pair of similar-bodied Regents was also built for East Midland Motor Services Ltd, but the general view was evidently that the resulting outline was rather too bizarre to be acceptable. It was withdrawn with almost all of Walsall's Regents in 1944.

The styling revolution that had been set in motion by the vehicles on the previous page was by no means immediately accepted. Quite apart from the more extreme cases of Halifax and Thomas Tilling, still placing open-staircase Regents in service into the early months of 1932, the piano-front type of front-end originally popularised in Britain by the Titan TD1 and still standard on the newly-introduced TD2 was quite widely regarded as an acceptably modern style. At Hull, a big intake of new buses for tram replacement included 20 Regents [16ft. 3in.] for which the body contract was split between Brush and English Electric. Seen here is the first of the Brush-bodied vehicles, No. 73 [RH 4761] on chassis 6611732.

City of Oxford Motor Services Ltd had placed 24 Regents with Park Royal bodywork in service in 1931, basically similar in appearance to the Nottingham vehicle shown on page 32, and a similar style was specified for six vehicles with Brush 48-seat bodywork placed in service early in 1932, No. 2 [JO 3762] on chassis 6611724 being shown. These vehicles had 100 mm bore engines and 15ft. 6½ in. wheelbase.

[Below] By 1932 the open-topped double-decker was rapidly becoming extinct. Most operators had abandoned the species as being too unsuitable for the British climate. However, an aptly-named London independent operator, Mr Charles Henry Pickup of Dulwich, considered the type sufficiently attractive to place five in service in the Spring and early Summer of 1932. They operated in central London on weekdays but on the more rural route 70 [Clapham-Dorking] on Sundays, the latter being to some degree the justification for them. Despite their traditional concept, Mr Pickup laid down an advanced specification for these buses. They were on the 16ft. 3in. chassis, the first such to operate in London, and the last one [6611846, registered GY 839] was among the first Regents to have vacuum-hydraulic brakes. The bodywork, built by Park Royal, was of up-to-date style with 56 seats [30 on the top deck], enclosed stairs and general appearance in the 1932 idiom apart from the open top. When London Transport took over the fleet in November 1933, these vehicles were given the fleet numbers STL553-557. The open-top concept did not appeal — perhaps the management had too vivid memories of the battle to obtain Police approval for operating covered-top double-deckers in the mid-'twenties — and the vehicles were given new covered top decks in 1935. This particular bus, GW 1224, on chassis 6611801 was the first, though numbered STL554. It was destroyed by fire as a result of an air raid when at Croydon garage in 1941, but the rest survived until 1948-50.

The period around 1932 was one of fascinating complexity as viewed from the standardised world of half-a-century later. When Dundee Corporation required rapid delivery of buses early in 1932, three stock chassis were supplied. One of these was 6611160, seen here, which had been ordered as one of the first 16ft. 3in. wheelbase demonstrators in March 1931 at the same time as 6611159, the Park Royal-bodied lightweight bus shown on page 33. The early history of this chassis is not known, but in August 1931 instructions were given to modify it to conform to a bodybuilder's drawing, possibly to suit the body shown, so it may simply have been retained for a time in chassis form for experimental purposes. Park Royal built two bodies to the design shown, the other going on to chassis 6611853, another of those ordered for the 1931 Olympia Show and these were placed in service at Dundee as Nos. 60 and 59 [TS 9862/1] respectively, early in 1932. The external body style was very similar to the original lightweight but these vehicles were 52-seaters, with 26 on the upper deck, and they differed in several details from that vehicle. The third vehicle, on chassis 6611842 had already been registered by AEC as MV 2271 and had a quite different Park Royal body [see page 55 of Park Royal Coachworks, Volume 1].

Another interesting divided order came from Northern General Transport Co Ltd of Gateshead. Of eight Regents with Brush bodywork new in July 1932, seven [6611909-1915] were 15ft. 6½in. wheelbase chassis with 52-seat bodywork to a recessed vee-front style not unlike the Walsall bus on page 34 but without the exaggerated vee effect. The eighth bus, No. 569 [CN 5247], was on 16ft. 3in. chassis, number 6611847, and had a 60-seat lightweight body of the AEC-design variety, as shown here. The seating arrangement is just visible in this view, with two rows of triple seats at the nearside rear of the upper-deck to bring the total upstairs to 34. Also evident is the curious rear-hinged cab door extending to the windscreen.

[Above] Morecambe and Heysham Corporation placed the body contract for its first fleet of six Regents with Weymann. The resulting design was clearly influenced by the 1931 AEC-design body, with its straight sloping profile and projecting cab front, although not so directly based on it as the contemporary Park Royal or Brush designs of this style. Weymann was to use this general profile for most of its output of such vehicles until the late 'thirties. The Morecambe vehicles were also up-to-date in providing accommodation for 56 passengers, but they had 100 mm engines and, like the Northern vehicle shown opposite, were supplied without electric starters, an amenity which, though taken for granted nowadays, was then not universally so regarded. The vehicles were delivered in March 1932, No. 34 [TF 7470], on chassis 6611816, being shown.

[Below] Subsequent production Weymann bodywork continued the same basic theme, but at first lacking a little of the sense of style of the original Morecambe version. These vehicles for Mansfield District Traction Co were part of a fleet of 30 similar 54-seat vehicles of which the first examples entered service in September 1932; there were also a further four Regents with Short Bros 56-seat bodies. The Weymann bodies had a more upright profile than those supplied to Morecambe, and also differed in having six-bay layout and shallower side panels. The chassis specification included vacuum-hydraulic brakes, a feature later adopted as standard. The leading vehicle seen here is No. 55 [VO 8555] the first of the Weymann batch on chassis 6611951, followed by Nos. 59, 56 and 62 of the same type. They remained in service until 1946-48. Note the provision of half cab doors only.

A long association with the South Wales Transport Co Ltd as a major operator of Regents began in 1932 when 50 examples with lowbridge Brush bodywork were placed in service. They were on basically standard petrol-engined chassis but had a system of allowing an extreme degree of tilt for the nearside headlamp, which accounts for its rather 'drunk' attitude in this picture of No. 26 [WN 4760] on chassis 6611879, the last vehicle in the first batch of twelve. The tall filler cap was as used on some LGOC vehicles at the time but the bonnet side panel, with a long row of vertical louvres, was to a newly adopted design used for provincial vehicles. The almost vertical driver's windscreen may also have been inspired by LGOC practice but gave rather a 'plain' appearance to this body style, usually associated with a raked screen. Some 24 of these vehicles were sold relatively early in life in 1938-39 but a high proportion saw further service, often rebodied. One of those retained had been fitted with an early example of the AEC 7.7-litre oil engine in November 1934.

With a new General Manager, W. Vane Morland, Leeds City Tramways and Transport Department became an AEC customer for the first time; the only previous example of the make operated had been an ex-World War I vehicle. Mr Vane Morland had come to Leeds from Walsall and there were obvious resemblances in the Walsall 1931 orders and those for Leeds in 1932, extending to the blue and cream livery and bodywork front-end styling despite the award of the bodybuilding contract for all the double-deckers locally to Charles H. Roe Ltd, which soon adopted this body design as its standard. There were a dozen Regents delivered in October-November, which were up-to-date in having 16ft. 3in. wheelbase chassis with vacuum-hydraulic brakes but the 100 mm engine was chosen and, as built, they lacked electric starters. One chassis, the first of the batch No. 40 [6611935], had fluid flywheel transmission, a feature which became standard at Leeds from 1934. The seating capacity was originally 55, with 29 on top, increased to 56 about 1937 when the gross weight restriction had been relaxed slightly. The entire batch were lent to London Transport in 1940-41 and No. 45 is seen passing Baker Street Underground station.

A batch of 23 Regents were ordered for delivery to London General Country Services Ltd soon after this organisation took over the East Surrey and other LGOC 'country' vehicles in April 1932. By that date the 16ft. 3in. wheelbase was officially standard and though quite a few orders for 15ft. 6½in. chassis were still going through for various operators, probably mainly for standardisation reasons, it must have been a specific decision that these were to be of the shorter type. The LGOC had placed no new Regents for its own fleet in service since the last of its ST-type had been delivered in June 1931, and its current standard new double-decker was the so-called 'Bluebird' [blue-upholstered] LT-type Renown six-wheeler seating 60. A shorter version of this style of body was produced for the LGCS vehicles. With the full-length upper-deck and right-angle stairs, the seating capacity could easily have been 52 but for some reason was kept down to 48, with 26 upstairs and only 22 down. A change of plan meant that only ten were placed in service immediately and some received three-letter Surrey [APC] registrations. They did not receive fleet numbers until 1935, when they became ST1032-9 and 1070-84. ST1074 [GX 5314], on the first chassis of the batch, 6612021, is seen in early post-war days.

[Above] Several of the larger South Wales independents were regular AEC customers in the 'thirties and D. Bassett & Sons [Gorseinon] Ltd took delivery of four Regents with fluid transmission in the winter of 1932-33. They were of 16ft. 3in. wheelbase and the Short Bros 54-seat bodywork, of the style that had been familiar on Regents for the previous couple of years or so, bears obvious evidence of being adapted to the new length, with 9in. or so of panelling at the rear of the lower-deck windows and a correspondingly lengthened rear dome upstairs. TG 4590, on chassis 6612124, later became United Welsh 581, being subsequently fitted with a Gardner 6LW engine and new East Lancs body.

[Right] The LGOC introduced its version of the 16ft. 3in. wheelbase Regent in December 1932, commencing a new class designation, STL [literally 'Short T Long'']. It followed up the 60-seat idea but unlike the AEC-design version of the previous winter, used a top deck built to almost the full length of the vehicle to allow satisfactory leg room for the 34 passengers seated there, and this projected more noticeably over the driver's windscreen than the Bluebird LT or ST shown opposite, though otherwise similar in outline. The design was simplified in other respects, largely to keep the weight down to 5 tons 18 cwt. The vehicle shown, STL 172 [66122317], is an example of the second batch and has the fully-floating rear axle, with larger hub, introduced during 1933, though also fitted on some earlier vehicles, originally including the first of this type, STL1.

Acceptance of the oil engine as a suitable power unit for buses was a relatively slow process and it is noteworthy that a handful of independent operators was among the limited numbers to place examples in service relatively early. The B & S Motor Service run by J. Bullock & Sons Ltd of Featherstone in the West Riding of Yorkshire was a rapidly expanding concern which added this Regent with 8.8-litre engine to its fleet in 1933. No. 149 [HL 5676] was based on chassis number 6612054 and had a Weymann 52-seat lowbridge body. The photograph was taken in Leeds a year or two later and also shows No. 161 [HL 6268], one of two Weymann-bodied AEC Q side-engined single-deckers and No. 171, a Daimler COG5 double-decker, both added to the fleet in 1934. Just visible over the roof of the Q is a Yorkshire [Woollen District] Titan with Brush body of the same period. The B & S business was taken over by West Riding Automobile Co Ltd in 1950, but the AEC vehicles shown had been withdrawn by then. The building behind the buses is the distinctively-named Leeds tram depot — Swinegate.

Chapter Four: The oil engine takes over.

AEC's pioneer work on road transport diesel engines took a little while to reach full fruition in terms of orders. The LGOC had steadily increased the proportion of oil-engined Renown six-wheeled double-deckers in successive orders in 1931-32. A total of 94 had AEC oil engines (including the three transferred from ST-type buses), plus a further eleven with the newly-introduced Gardner 6LW unit. There were fewer than a couple of dozen oil-engined Regents in service anywhere at the end of 1932, but the position was soon to change.

From the end of 1932, the oil-engined Regent, which at that time had the A165 8.8-litre engine, began to win more orders, especially from municipalities. Halifax placed seven in service, Bury ten, and Reading, one, while other users included such independent operators as Baillie Bros of Dumbarton, with three, and J. Bullock & Sons of Featherstone, in the West Riding, with one. Other examples went out on an experimental or demonstration basis to such operators as Sheffield and Leeds.

The LGOC could not accommodate the 8.8-litre engine in its new 60-seat STL buses without a reduction in body length and, more important, some sacrifice of seating due mainly to the increased weight. So all were petrol, the choice remaining with the 100 mm unit, by then no longer even mentioned in AEC publicity material which quoted only the 110 mm high-power head 120 bhp engine. Understandably the Tilling STL buses, ordered through LGOC as Tilling prepared to wind up its London operations, were the same. There were originally to have been 102 of these and LGOC allocated the fleet numbers STL51-152 though the order was later reduced and the last 22 numbers never filled. Hence when LGOC ordered a further 100 chassis, 6612298-2397, they took the numbers STL153-252. The first 50 were 60-seat buses almost identical to STL1-49, but STL203-252 marked a further step towards the typical London bus of the mid and late 'thirties, with fluid flywheels, Daimler-built pre-selective gearboxes and 56-seat Chiswick-built bodywork, the latter now having a sloping front. They entered service during the summer of 1933 which also saw the transfer of LGOC and Tilling's London operations to the new London Passenger Transport Board.

However, LGOC had ordered but not received another 100 Regents, which appeared as STL253-352, and indeed a total of 200 chassis numbers were evidently allocated at that time, for 6612473-2672 were STL 253-452 in order. The first 39 were similar to the previous type, with petrol engines, Daimler transmission and almost identical bodywork. But the next 50, STL292-341, received 110 mm petrol engines

Thomas Tilling's interpretation of the 16ft. 3in. wheelbase Regent for London service also took shape in the latter part of 1932 and, in execution, was slightly in front of that of the LGOC, even though the allocation of chassis numbers [LGOC 6612071-2120, Tilling 6612164-2243] implies that it had been intended that the LGOC buses should be first. It had been agreed that the vehicles were to be given fleet numbers within LGOC's system and this photograph shows that the first vehicle was actually signwritten with the fleet number ST 837 on the front dumb-irons, which was the first vacant number in the ST series at that time. It is not clear whether it was originally the intention to number these buses [and presumably by implication the LGOC 60-seat buses and other later Regents] in the ST class or whether there had simply been a breakdown of communications somewhere, but YY 5351 was quickly renumbered STL51 [the registration number matching the last two figures, significantly] and the Tilling vehicles continued the series to STL 130. Tilling's body design, executed in its own works, was very similar to that for its earlier buses so far as the lower deck was concerned, but a much more modern-looking top deck with sloping frontal profile and enclosed stairs was used, with seating for 56 [30 up, 26 down]. After the London-based Tilling fleet was taken over by London Transport in October 1933, they remained at the former Tilling garages at Bromley, Catford and Croydon, some 20 being destroyed by fire at Croydon during an air raid in 1941. All remained petrol-engined throughout their lives.

removed from LT-type Renowns which were being converted with new 8.8-litre A165 oil engines and, like them, had conventional 'crash' gearboxes. The 8.8-litre engine's extra length caused no problem for the LT-class buses which were well within the 30ft. length limit applicable to six-wheel buses and offered greater fuel savings on these heavier vehicles. The final eleven vehicles of this batch, STL342-352, also with Daimler-built gearboxes, had some of the first examples of a new 7.7-litre oil engine, to be described more fully in the next chapter. The next 49 buses, STL353-402, were further vehicles with ex-LT petrol engines and crash gearboxes, but the last 50 of the 200, STL403-452, and also a further 150 buses STL453-552 and 559-608 (6612773-2872 and 2974-3023), although also having ex-LT petrol engines, had preselective transmission. The gearboxes in this case were of a new type made by AEC, and distinguishable in sound from the Daimler version no doubt due to slightly different gear profiles, but incorporating the same Wilson-designed principles.

Delivery of these sloping-front 56-seat STL buses, which thus totalled 400, were spread over about a year, ending in the summer of 1934. With the previous 100 60-seat LGOC buses, some 500 new Regents had thus been added to the LGOC/London

Transport fleet in about a year and a half, and Regent chassis numbers had advanced by 953. The total ultimate content for the London Transport fleet brought its proportion of Regent output in this period rather higher to about 61%, as in addition to the 80 Tilling STL's, a dozen were built for the country department of London Transport which had succeeded London General Country Services but at first continued some of its practices. These vehicles entered service in the Spring of 1934, at first without fleet numbers, and were unusual among London Regents in several respects. They had lowbridge Weymann bodywork of that firm's newly-introduced metal-framed type based on Metro-Cammell patents (the two firms having set up a joint sales organisation), and were of front-entrance layout, then beginning a run of limited popularity for double-deckers. They also had 8.8-litre oil engines and were to remain the only London Transport Regents so fitted, apart from a few brief experimental installations. Their chassis numbers, O6612271-2282, have misled some into thinking that they had older chassis than the second batch of LGOC 60-seat buses which began at 6612298, but it seems clear that they were issued with numbers that were left blank, very possibly from the cancelled Tilling STL order.

To confuse the issue further, they ultimately received the fleet numbers STL1044-1055 (not in order) in 1935, thereafter becoming generally known as the Godstone STLs.

Provincial customers during this period included regular customers such as Oxford (for whom the first Weymann metal-framed body had been built in 1933 on 6612125), Huddersfield, Nottingham, Halifax and Westcliff. The output of 8.8-litre oil-engined Regents received a big boost in the winter of 1933-34, when 30 with Weymann metal-bodies for tramway replacement at Rhondda were immediately followed numerically by 24 similar chassis with Short Bros bodies for Devon General. From about this date, most orders were for oil-engined buses and although London Transport was still putting petrol Regents into service, the supply of truly new ones had ceased in 1933 — the parallel conversions of LT-class Renowns meant that Regent chassis less engines and separate 8.8-litre engines were being produced in balanced numbers. A few customers were still taking petrol buses, mainly in areas such as seaside or other resorts where the quieter running of the petrol engine was still preferred, such as Morecambe, Wallasey, Westcliff, Cheltenham and Douglas (Isle of Man).

Another early user of oil-engined Regents was Baillie Bros Ltd of Dumbarton, which placed three in service in the earlier part of 1933. Two had 52-seat low-height bodywork by Roe, including No. 52 [SN 5855] on chassis 6612137, photographed in October 1934 when passing the Kelvin Hall used for Scottish Motor Shows. The body design on these vehicles was unlike that of any other Roe product, though it resembled that of the Cowieson body on the third vehicle. The Baillie Bros fleet was taken over by Central SMT in 1936.

[Below] Demonstrators were sent out from Southall in considerable numbers in the 'thirties. This oil-engined example with Park Royal low-height bodywork seen being tilt-tested at what had by then become London Transport's Chiswick works in October 1933 was painted in the livery of Plymouth Corporation, its bodywork being not unlike that by the same bodybuilder on some Dennis Lance double-deckers supplied in 1931. It is believed to have been AML 272 [O6612267] which was also demonstrated to Coventry. No Regent orders came in as a result of either visit, though Coventry did specify the 8.8-litre engine for some Daimler COA6 double-deckers supplied the following year. The chassis ultimately became a single-deck coach with post-1945 body by West-Nor, in the fleet of Silvertown Coaches. In the background can be seen various types of London Transport ex-LGOC bodywork removed from their chassis for overhaul and still bearing the General fleet name retained until 1934.

Exports of Regent chassis were few in numbers in the early days but in February 1933 an order was fulfilled for four for Madrid Tramways. This vehicle was one of three with petrol engines [6612059-61], the fourth having an oil engine and fluid transmission [6612132], all having 54-seat bodywork by Park Royal, built with platform on the right and to an overall width of about 8ft. though the only chassis feature of any consequence departing from the home-market standard was the left-hand exhaust outlet. Strictly speaking these were ACLO Regents, the AEC name not being used in Spanish-speaking countries. The radiator, hub cap and the transfer on the Autovac unit all had ACLO lettering.

For the most part, major British operating companies, except in Scotland, still tended to take a very cautious line on the adoption of the diesel, or as it was still usually called, oil-engined bus. Even relatively progressive companies such as Northern General Transport Co Ltd, busy at the time with its own design of side-engined single-decker, still chose petrol engines for it and an almost equally adventurous type of double-decker. Short Bros had introduced what was described as the 'Dustless double-decker' on a Regent chassis in the Autumn of 1932 and NGT placed three examples in service in June 1933, including No. 574 [CN 5507] on chassis 6612144, seen here at Southall before delivery. These were low-height buses, with stairs running across the front bulkhead — seating was provided for 27 upstairs and 26 below. The angling of the window at the nearside of the bulkhead was intended to produce an extraction effect to avoid draughts if the bus was operated with the door open.

A new AEC customer was Douglas Corporation on the Isle of Man, hitherto a user of Tilling-Stevens petrol-electric buses. No. 42 [MN 8691] on chassis 6612147 was one of the first two Regents to be supplied and is seen here bearing publicity lettering "Off to Douglas — shall I meet you there" for the delivery trip across the Irish Sea in time for the 1933 Summer season. Petrol-engined chassis were chosen and the bodywork was built by Northern Counties Motor & Engineering Co Ltd to that concern's newly-introduced metal-framed standard mid-'thirties design. Ultimately a fleet of ten similar Regents was built up by 1939. Note that no provision for destination displays appears to have been made.

Also operating within sight of the Irish Sea, three more petrol Regents were supplied in 1933 to Morecambe & Heysham Corporation. They again had Weymann bodywork but this time also of metal-framed construction, following the agreement setting up the MCW organisation jointly-owned with Metro-Cammell, whose constructional system was used. The vehicle shown, No. 35 [TJ 2490] on chassis 6612245 had body number M17 in the Weymann metal-framed body series beginning at M1. This body design was to be used by Weymann until the late 'thirties.

The Oxford fleet's intake of fourteen Regents during 1933 included one with Brush 52-seat bodywork on chassis 6612248, as shown. The styling of this particular vehicle was of an unusual interim style with, basically, the straight sloping profile above the rounded projecting cab front that had become increasingly fashionable since first seen on the AEC-design lightweight body style of 1931. However, not all tastes had accepted this style and here Brush married it with the projecting roof as favoured in more typical 1931 designs. The Oxford company had by this date introduced its prefix letter system, G signifying the AEC Regent with standard crash gearbox, though there was only one vehicle numbered 25 in the fleet. In 1946, the classified prefix system was dropped except that H was used to signify 'highbridge'. This vehicle was withdrawn in 1948 but remained in passenger service with Cottrell of Mitcheldean near Gloucester until 1960 and even then continued for some years as a lorry.

Up to 1933, a high proportion of the oil-engined Regents built had been 'one-offs', either built on a speculative basis as demonstrators or purchased by operators partly in order to gain experience of the still unfamiliar type of engine. The vehicle shown, O6612398, was another case in point, being purchased by Aberdare UDC as its fleet number 1 and registered TG 6565. Park Royal built the bodywork to what had been adopted as its standard design, reverting very closely to the AEC 1931 lightweight prototype in outline, with five bays and a well-raked front to the upper-deck. The 8.8-litre engine's lively performance might have been expected to suit the hills of the operating area, but Aberdare turned to the considerably less powerful but doubtless more economical Daimler COG5 for most of its subsequent bus orders in the 'thirties.

[Below] However, in the same area something of a breakthrough was achieved with the first major order from a BET-associated company for oil-engined Regents. The Rhondda Tramways Co Ltd chose this model for a fleet of 30 double-deckers placed in service to replace the company's trams in December 1933 and January 1934. They had Weymann metal-framed bodywork seating 52 [28 up, 24 down], the design having a slightly more upright front-end than the Morecambe version. The second vehicle of the order, on chassis O6612406, is seen on a

misty day before leaving Southall. At the same time an order came in from another BET subsidiary, Devon General for 24 vehicles [similar to that shown on page 49] and so, quite suddenly, the 8.8 Regent had

'arrived', for municipal orders were also gaining momentum. Although a few of the Rhondda vehicles were withdrawn in 1945, twenty of them lasted until the 'fifties and the last four until 1955.

Two quite different types of vehicle placed in service by the London Passenger Transport Board within its first year are shown on this page. Above is seen LGOC's final design of bodywork for the Regent chassis, abandoning the concept of maximum possible seating capacity for the increasingly-preferred 56-seat bus with sloping profile. Somehow the details of the front-end styling did not produce a particularly attractive overall effect, lacking the character of the 60-seat version or the harmonious profile of the version introduced in August 1934. STL257, on chassis 6612477, was one of a batch of 39 buses with fluid flywheels and Daimler-built preselective gearboxes ordered by LGOC but placed in service towards the end of 1933, after the LPTB had taken over. They had petrol engines removed from LT-type AEC Renown six-wheelers then being fitted with new 8.8-litre oil engines. The latter engines could not have been accommodated on the STL buses without a reduction in

seating capacity, though these STLs received 7.7-litre oil engines on flexible mountings in 1939. The photograph was taken at Victoria Station; the LPTB retained the traditional General fleetname at first.

For the special circumstances of the 410 service operated by Godstone garage in the country area, however, a batch of twelve 8.8-litre oil-engined Regents with crash gearboxes was supplied in the Spring of 1934. These had low-height 48-seat Weymann metal-framed bodywork with front-entrance layout, the doorway design resembling that introduced in 1932 by Short Bros. They had few London characteristics but had a certain purposeful air about them. At first, they operated without fleet numbers, though by the time this delightfully atmospheric photographic study of a wet day in Reigate was taken around 1938, BPF 417 had become STL1052.

Front view of a Regent chassis with 8.8-litre A165 oil engine, as being built towards the end of 1933. By that date, the oil engine had finally 'arrived' and AEC officially regarded it as standard and the petrol unit as the optional alternative [at reduced cost] with effect from November of that year. A Regent chassis as shown cost £1,425, according to published price lists, if the standard 'crash' gearbox was fitted, an extra £100 being charged for fluid transmission [ie the fluid flywheel and pre-selective gearbox, still at that date being bought out from Daimler]. Vacuum-hydraulic brakes, using Lockheed equipment, was standard. The petrol versions were £300 cheaper. These prices made the Regent about the most expensive conventional two-axle model available, but in practice substantial discounts were often offered, especially for large orders, in those highly competitive days.

The photograph shows the typical Regent radiator of the 1930-37 period, mounted slightly higher than on petrol models when the 8.8 oil engine was fitted [as well as further forward, though that is not evident in this view]. The 'Oil Engine' title was used from 1931 until shortly after the 7.7-litre engine became standard, around 1936. It was evidently considered that a starting handle had become of little practical value with a high-compression oil engine of this size — AEC did not fit any form of decompression device as found on some Gardner engines at this period. Note the aluminium mudguard, light but perhaps not so good at withstanding minor knocks as the early steel type. Wiring was provided for a wing-mounted sidelamp but it was not fitted until at the bodybuilders — the wing-edge marker to aid driver judgement in manoeuvring was a characteristic AEC feature from 1931 to about 1937.

The A165 engine, with its 130 bhp output, gave the oil-engined Regent outstanding performance in its day — the nearest approach in terms of power among contemporary oil engines in volume production in the early 'thirties was the 102 bhp given by the Gardner 6LW, though admittedly the maximum torque did not differ so widely. The Halifax area, with its long gradients, gave the '8.8' ideal opportunity to demonstrate its capabilities, and the municipal transport fleet standardised on it almost exclusively from 1933 until 1939. Here No. 142 [JX 1915] of the Halifax Joint Committee's fleet tackles a typical climb. Delivered in July 1934, it had Roe 51-seat bodywork on chassis O6612713, and was photographed later that year.

Great Yarmouth Corporation placed seven Regents in service in June-July 1934, all with A165 8.8-litre oil engines and bodywork by English Electric, with the conservative seating capacity by that date of 48. The body design was English Electric's standard style from 1932, when the Hull Regents bodied by this concern to a basically similar design appeared, followed by a batch for Bournemouth with rear entrance and front exit layout. No. 33 [EX 3472] on chassis O6612720 is seen above, with holiday visitors boarding, soon after delivery. The vehicle following is one of Great Yarmouth's Guy BB-type single-deckers of the 'twenties, with United bodywork.

The scene below, taken in Manchester the following winter contrasted with that above in several respects other than the weather. Arthur Mayne ran a service connecting the city centre and the area near his Droylsden garage among the inner suburbs to the east of the city. The Regent shown, 6612771, had just been added to the fleet in November 1934. Taking advantage of the weight saving and more compact front-end given by using a petrol-engined chassis, he was able to achieve a 60-passenger seating capacity despite the use of the front entrance layout hitherto associated with some loss of space — in this case a compact staircase and entrance layout helped. Park Royal built the body and three more similar vehicles, but with no less than 62 seats — then the highest capacity of any two-axle motor buses in Britain — entered service in 1935-36, followed by the rebodying of an ex-Nottingham 1929 Regent chassis in similar manner in 1938, AXJ 496 also being modified to seat 62. Oddly enough, little publicity was given to this remarkable venture at the time.

Across the other side of Manchester, in Salford, the municipal transport fleet was also putting Regents on the road for the first time in 1934. However, this undertaking tended to follow a conservative policy, apart from the adoption of the oil engine, for the six vehicles involved seated only 48 [26 up, 22 down] in their metal-framed bodywork. This was built by Metro-Cammell to a style supplied to several operators in the 'thirties, noticeably more angular than the Weymann versions using the same form of construction, though having its own well-proportioned visual appeal. Salford was to receive several further batches on Regent [all 8.8-litre] and other chassis throughout the 'thirties. This one was No. 117 [O6612764].

The drawback to the 8.8-litre engine — the effect of its length on body space — is conveyed in this photograph of an example with Short Bros 52-seat [28 up, 24 down] body supplied to Devon General in May 1935, No. 225 [AUO 91] on chassis O6612940 being one of a repeat order for two vehicles added to a fleet of 24 virtually identical vehicles supplied in 1933-34. The body design — much less severe in outline than some other Short double-deckers of the period — was quite similar to some being supplied on Leyland Titan chassis to Southdown Motor Services on Leyland Titan TD3 chassis at that time. However, on the 8.8-litre Regent the rearmost windows were shortened by about the 4½ in. or so by which the radiator projected forward to keep within the 26ft. overall length. Short Bros evidently preferred to retain its standard body size framing and window dimensions as far as possible, rather than respacing the pillars. However, these were well-liked and successful vehicles, all 26 being either rebodied by Brush or rebuilt, retaining the 8.8-litre engines which proved well suited to Devon's hilly terrain, in 1947-51. This one, rebodied in 1949, remained in service until 1957, along with most of the type. Short Bros was fading from its position of prominence as a bus bodybuilder, reverting to its original role as an aircraft maker with the upsurge of interest in flying boats — only about a dozen more Regents were bodied by Short susbequently.

The availability of the 7.7-litre engine in the Regent chassis enabled London Transport to pursue its aim of standardising on a chassis so equipped that would accept an equally standard 56-seat body. Curiously, having achieved this goal, it promptly introduced a variation of the theme — the country area front-entrance version. However, there was much in common between the red central area rear-entrance bus in the form introduced in August 1934 and the green country area version shown in this photograph taken six months later. The chassis now all had fluid transmission, with preselective gearboxes made at the AEC works, and the outline of the bodywork was the same except for the entrance position, which again was of the design with angled left-hand edge of the front bulkhead and correspondingly angled panel at the rear of the entrance. This occupied more space than a conventional entrance at either front or rear, but no attempt was made to obtain maximum seating capacity, which was for 29 on the top deck and only nineteen below, giving a total of 48.

Considerable attention was now being paid to appearance by London Transport which was getting into its stride and seeking to set high standards in all fields. A new gently curved profile was possibly inspired by that of the Q-type double-deckers despite London Transport's lack of enthusiasm for other aspects of their design. However, detail features were also given close scrutiny and LT introduced new designs of front mudguard [extending lower at the front than the contemporary AEC standard and more rounded, with a reverse curve at the rear, not unlike pre-1931 Leyland styles], and bonnet [having no louvres] as well as adopting a gentle curve for the lower edge of the driver's windscreen and bulkhead window — chassis for LT were supplied without dash panels. STL963, on chassis O6613251, was one of 85 front-entrance Regents bodied by the LPTB at Chiswick immediately after the first 150 central area buses of similar profile. Both originally had the small rectangular side-lights shown, built into the black strip at upper-deck floor level.

Chapter Five: The arrival of the '7.7'

The main breakthrough in 1934 was the introduction of a new oil engine, type A171, that would fit in the standard front-end, directly in place of the petrol engine, instead of requiring a longer bonnet and thus causing loss of precious inches of the still restrictive 26ft. overall length limit, as was the case with the 8.8-litre A165 unit. The A171 was actually derived from the entirely new oil engine developed for the AEC Q side-engined bus (see Best of British Buses No. 2), having bore and stroke dimensions of 106 mm by 146 mm and a swept volume of 7.7-litres. Early in production, the bore was reduced by 1 mm and the swept volume thus became 7.58-litres, but AEC's publicity machine had become addicted to 1.1-litre steps in engine sizes and the "seven seven" had already become part of the language among bus engineers. The design retained the Ricardo indirect-injection system which if not as economical as the best direct-injection engines allowed a good power output, usually 115 bhp at 2,000 rpm. This was ample for most fleets in the 'thirties.

However, AEC proceeded cautiously and a dozen engines were supplied initially to London Transport, eleven going into STL342-352 as already mentioned and one being used to convert an early open-staircase Renown, LT21. No announcement of the availability of the 7.7-litre engine in a form suitable for the Regent or other front-engined chassis was made at that stage and the standard AEC oil engine for these models continued to be the 8.8-litre A165 unit.

In passing, it is noteworthy that the availability of a Regent 4 model — i.e. a Regent with four-cylinder engine — was regularly mentioned in the brief data sheet which formed part of AEC's monthly house magazine 'AEC Gazette' in the 1932-34 period. No further details, beyond the availability of oil or petrol versions from 1933, were quoted and none were built, though it is self-evident that it would have been a double-decker equivalent of model 642, the Regal 4 (see Best of British Buses No. 6). No model number was allocated, and it could not have been 641 as this was already occupied by Monarch and Mercury goods chassis — indeed

various four-cylinder goods models took the series to 648.

Leeds leads

The earliest provincial user of the 7.7-litre engine in Regent chassis was Leeds City Transport, which, like London Transport, had adopted Regent chassis with preselective gearboxes and 56-seat bodywork as its standard, although the bodywork was locally built by Roe. Such a seating capacity was still above average and required careful attention to weight reduction to be possible within the gross weight limit then in force. A batch of 31 Regents, registered ANW 670-700, was completed by Roe between August and October 1934. Official coachbuilder's records show them to have been 56-seaters and to have had 'plain' chassis numbers 6612732-62 (rather than the 'O' prefix numbers used by then for oil-engined chassis) and there is no mention of 'CI' (indicating 'compression-ignition') as was Roe's practice for diesel buses at that date. However, all but the first seven were delivered to LCT with oil engines, so were probably converted after body-building by AEC, acquiring O prefix numbers in the process and

losing a pair of seats on the upper-deck at the same time, and the remainder were converted by March 1935. No other 7.7-litre Regents appear to have been built for provincial operators until 1935.

However, at about the same time as the first of the ANW-registered Leeds buses, London Transport was placing its first examples of what was to prove in retrospect the basic standard type of STL in service, also with 7.7-litre engines and fluid transmission. A new design of 56-seat Chiswick-built body had been introduced, with gently curving front profile, unbroken from cab front to roof, and although rather spartan in some respects, London Transport had set a new standard for styling as well as mechanical design. The first 150 followed on from the previous batch, beginning at STL609 (O6613024) and continuing in sequence to STL758. The standard oil-engined STL was a nimble bus, with ample power, particularly as originally built, and the quick and simple gearchanges possible with the preselective gearbox.

A new data sheet, issued in April 1935, quoted the 105 x 146 mm engine size (ie the '7.7') for all six-cylinder oil-engined AEC passenger models, making no mention of the 115 x 142 mm (8.8-litre) size until

The standard oil-engined Regent, as supplied to provincial customers [ie other than London Transport], now looked almost identical with the petrol version, retaining the 'sharp-edged' front wings and with unpainted radiator stoneguard, unlike the LT black-painted version. The more compact 7.7-litre engine no longer needed the forward-mounted radiator and, indeed, the bonnet top and side panels became the same as used for the contemporary petrol model. The example with standard crash gearbox, seen here, was probably photographed soon after the A171 unit was adopted as standard, during 1935. This Ricardo-head indirect-injection 7.7 engine can be distinguished from the later A173 direct-injection version by its single full-length rocker cover [the A173 having two separate covers to suit the separate cylinder heads each covering three cylinders]. Generally oil-engined chassis did not have starting handles, though a few operators evidently still specified them, possibly for maintenance reasons.

then standard. Even the cost of a Regent with oil engine and standard gearbox, a decidedly pricey £1,425, had not altered since the previous September. AEC publicity seems to have made no 'splash' about the changeover, despite the practical benefit given by the 7.7-litre engine's compactness. In practice, deliveries of 7.7-litre Regents for operators in general began to come through from about June 1935, though Leeds managed to get in early a second time with another 40, this time with 7.7-litre engines from the start, of which delivery began in April.

Clearly, some people, at least, at AEC expected the 8.8-litre engine to die — an understandable attitude, since the 115 bhp output from the 7.7-litre engine was about the highest of any diesel bus in regular production in Britain at the time. But it didn't work out as simply as that. The 8.8-litre engine, if not as economical as some of its competitors, had built up a reputation for reliability. And in some types of operation at least, the need to use the gearbox more with the 7.7 made the latter little if any more economical.

Municipalities, in particular, tended to divide into those switching to the 7.7 after 1935, such as Leeds, Cardiff, Bradford, Reading and West Bridgford, and those continuing to specify the 8.8, such as Sheffield, Halifax, Rochdale and Salford. The

BET companies in general changed over immediately and new customers naturally tended to accept the latest standard model, notably Liverpool Corporation, with an impressive first order for 42 Regents with 7.7 engines and Weymann bodywork in 1936 after several years of not buying new buses.

London Transport placed further orders for STL chassis with 7.7-litre A171 engines and preselective gearboxes, having arrived at a specification which met its needs and was to continue to do so until 1938. The main 1935 order was for 285 chassis (O6613247-3531) of which the first 85 were for the country department, and had bodies built by LTPB itself at Chiswick to the standard curved-profile outline established the previous year but with front entrance position and 48-seat capacity. These green-painted vehicles received the fleet numbers STL959-1043, and were followed by standard red central area vehicles STL759-958. A further four country STL buses on an individual batch of chassis O6613648-51 took numbers STL1056-1059 immediately after the Godstone STLs. The next main batch of 200 buses, all 56-seat red buses, were O6613793-3992, STL1060-1259, but another group of four extras, O6613714-8 had meanwhile been built in a curiously elaborate exercise to take the LGOC bodywork from the three pioneer 1930

Daimler CH6 buses which had introduced fluid flywheel transmission to the LGOC, plus one similar chassis acquired from the Redline company. These chassis had a special wheelbase to avoid any need to rebuild the bodies but were numbered STL1260-3, entering service in April 1936.

Meanwhile a further engine development had occurred. To meet the growing challenge of competitive direct-injection engines, and in particular the Gardner 5LW unit, a new version of the A171 7.7-litre unit designated A173 was introduced. This adopted direct-injection, of a type using a toroidal cavity in the piston, giving a useful gain in economy at the cost of reduced power — early examples gave 90 bhp at 1750 rpm, both figures being slightly more than the 85 bhp at 1700 then produced by the 5LW.

AEC acted rather shyly in regard to this toroidal engine and although this was later explained to the outside world as a wish for it to be proved in service before making a public announcement, there were sharp differences of opinion at Southall. The engine design chief, C. B. Dicksee, by then quite eminent, favoured the indirect-injection Ricardo-head engine, with its better power output and, it was claimed, lower demands on fuel quality and filtration. The direct-injection engine had been developed by a member of his staff and it was clear that some operators, at least, were liable to place orders elsewhere unless AEC could equal its competitors' fuel economy. So a compromise was reached, with the new A173 engine being offered and demonstrated to likely customers, but with no publicity for the time being.

Among the earliest Regents with this unit was a demonstrator, O6613792, built in 1936 with Park Royal bodywork and registered EML 876 before being supplied to Newcastle Corporation, which operated it on loan for about a year in grey livery. It had fluid transmission and the aim was clearly to recapture the business which had been lost to Daimler with the Gardner 5LW-engined COG5. It still didn't quite succeed in meeting the fuel economy of this model, so Daimler got Newcastle's orders for 1937-39. However, the vehicle was purchased and repainted in standard dark blue livery, to the delight of the author, already an AEC enthusiast at the age of 11, though he wasn't aware of the engine story until many years later.

Nottingham Corporation had stayed with the A165 8.8-litre unit for its first two 1936 Regent batches, but later in the year switched to the 7.7 and it is believed that these latter vehicles were also of direct-injection type from new. Certainly by early 1937, Regents with A173 engines were becoming commonplace, including 50 buses purchased by Swansea Improvements & Tramways Co for tramway replacement and subsequently incorporated in the South Wales fleet, O6614971-5020.

However, London Transport, which was buying in bigger batches, remained loyal to the A171 unit. Thus not only the 350 vehicles O6614031-4380 (STL 1264-1513), of which the last 50 were another 50 front-entrance country area buses bodied this time by Weymann to LPTB style but with metal frames, were of this chassis type, but also the 500 with chassis O6614446-4945 (STL1514-2013) built in 1936-37. All but the last three of a further 502 built in 1937-38 were 'more of the same' so far as the chassis were concerned, O6615441-5942, but the first 175, STL2014-2188, had Park Royal-built metal-framed bodies to

standard central area pattern, the rest being bodied at Chiswick.

Analysing the total of no less than 2,919 chassis numbers covered during 1934-38 by the range between O6613024, STL609, the first 'standard' STL and the end of the 1937-38 STL batch, O6615942, some 1,995 chassis had been supplied to London Transport, almost all to a standardised design, with the A171 7.7-litre engine and fluid transmission, to add to the original eleven placed in service earlier in 1934. The remaining 924 built during this period were mostly for well-established AEC customers, including mainly municipalities and BET companies, plus one or two independent concerns standardising on Regents in modest numbers. However, they did include more export examples than hitherto, with several orders for Australia. Most were oil-engined, and although a diminishing handful of operators were still taking petrol-engined Regents the switch to diesel was much more complete by 1938 than among the corresponding Regal single-deckers.

AEC switched to the recently-introduced standard Park Royal metal-framed body for some of its early 7.7-litre Regent demonstrators. This one on chassis O6612577 was registered as DHX 125 and sent to Aberdeen Corporation in 1936. As was often the case with such vehicles, it was purchased by the Corporation after a few months, becoming No. 107, and was to have a remarkably long life, not being withdrawn until 1959. Aberdeen chose the 7.7-litre engine for some Regal single-deckers but favoured the Daimler COG6 [of which a demonstrator example was also purchased in 1936] for double-deckers until 1939, when some 8.8-litre Regents were purchased. DHX 125 was photographed in service, later in 1936. The London-registered Ford 8 in the foreground, probably a sales rep's car and a few months old at the time, would have cost its owner £100 — AEC's extra charge for fluid transmission at the time was £125. Evident in the background, in addition to three Corporation trams and the rear of a Crossley double-decker, are two Rover saloons and a Morris 8 tourer, all locally registered.

Despite AEC's switch to the 7.7-litre engine as the standard Regent power unit, some operators decided that the 8.8-litre unit suited their needs better. This example for the Sheffield fleet was placed in service in June 1935 and may have been ordered before the changeover, but the A165 8.8-litre engine was to remain standard for this fleet's sizeable intake of Regents until the wartime era. The bodywork was in most cases by Weymann either of the style shown or a later development of it with curved profile. The vehicle shown, No. 103 [BWA 203] on chassis O6613547 was part of the Sheffield Corporation and LMS and LNE Railways Joint Committee fleet, this vehicle being one of those owned by the London Midland & Scottish Railway Company. The seating capacity was 53, an unusual total for a conventional centre-gangway double-decker, with 29 upstairs and 24 down, no doubt to conform to the contemporary gross weight limit — later buses seated 55 or 56.

One of the stranger London Transport decisions was that providing for special new chassis to be built to accept the bodywork from the three Daimler CH6 buses that had been bought by the LGOC in October 1930 to try out the then new fluid flywheel and preselective gearbox, plus one other CH6 acquired from an independent operator, E. Brickwood Ltd. The ex-LGOC buses, which had been numbered DST1-3, had LGOC-built bodywork virtually identical to that on an ST. The transmission had been highly successful but London Transport found the sleeve-valve engines troublesome. However, instead of simply replacing the engines with AEC units, either petrol [as had been done on the similarly powered ADC LS-type six-wheelers] or 7.7-litre oil, or merely adding the bodies to the float for the ST class [which would probably not have been too difficult, as the CH6 wheelbase was almost identical to that of the ST] four new chassis of current STL specification [7.7-litre oil engines and preselective transmission] but with special short wheelbase were produced. Logically they should have been numbered ST1140-43, but instead they appeared in April 1936 as STL1260-4. STL 1261 is seen at Victoria in 1949, together with, on the right, one of 180 new Bristol K-type buses 'borrowed' by London Transport at that time, in this case from United Counties.

Among provincial operators which switched from 8.8 to 7.7-litre versions of the Regent in line with the change in AEC's standard specification was Bradford Corporation — the 1935 batch of 25 having the larger engine and the 1936 delivery of ten having the latter. In both cases the body contract was split between Weymann and English Electric but preselective gearboxes were standardised. The vehicle shown, No. 425 [AKW 425] of the 1936 batch, was on chassis O6614047 — the zig-zag edging of the metal louvre over the windows was a Bradford peculiarity but the body design was in other respects a typical Weymann metal-framed product of the period — seating was provided for 54 passengers [28 up, 26 down]. The 'Bradford' fleetname underlined except under the larger first and last letters was unusual among municipal fleets at that date, having a style more associated with company undertakings.

Green's Motors Ltd of Haverfordwest was operating a fleet of about fifteen vehicles mainly of Leyland make and including two Titans on thirteen routes in the Milford Haven and Tenby area when this Regent, BDE 370, on standard 7.7-litre chassis O6614052, was added to the fleet in 1936. The Park Royal lowbridge body was of the metal-framed type and seated 53 with 27 upstairs and 26 down. It was evidently doing good business when photographed soon after entering service. Note the coloured light fitted under the destination indicator to aid identification by intending passengers — quite a common idea in those days of numerous operators. A single-decker on Regal chassis was also supplied.

By 1936, the production of London Transport STL-type in what had already become regarded as the standard style was not only well under way but growing in pace. Chassis were being ordered in larger batches, and STL1301, seen here when new early in 1936, had chassis O6614168 which was one of a batch of 350, of which 300 were 56-seat rear-entrance central area buses of the type illustrated, with bodywork built by LPTB at Chiswick (STL1264-1463) and 50 were country area buses with 48-seat front-entrance bodywork outwardly similar to that shown on page 50 but of Weymann metal-framed construction. They were followed by batches of no less than 500 and then 502 chassis, all of which were built as central area rear-entrance buses. There were variations of destination indicator layout and 40 buses were of a special design for operation through Blackwall Tunnel, but with earlier batches built from 1934 onwards there were, by 1938, over 1500 STL buses of this general style and bodied at Chiswick on the road. The neat and functional appearance helped to build up the image of London Transport as an imaginative organisation with high standards of taste and the lively performance was well suited to the need for brief periods of brisk running to make up time lost in London's traffic, growing even in those days. The passenger's impression was slightly let down by the use of light green paint on the window trim, where the grain revealed that this was of wood. Indeed the general quality of the timber-framed bodywork, though quite adequate for their intended life with LPTB's normal peacetime standards of maintenance, was not to prove as durable as the best metal-framed (or for that matter teak-framed) products of the period. The front and rear wheel discs shown on this particular bus — quite possibly the reason for the photograph — were not standard, though they were to be used on later London Transport vehicles. Note the lack of cab door, which remained a feature of London's double-deckers until the wartime era, except for the RT class.

The front-entrance double-decker was quite fashionable in certain parts of Britain in the 'thirties, none more so than the East Midlands. This 1937 AEC Regent with 7.7-litre engine in the Midland General Omnibus Co Ltd fleet was photographed at Huntingdon Street Bus Station in Nottingham in August 1939 and, although only partially visible, all the double-decker motor buses in the background were also of this layout. MGO's No. 4 [DNU 953] on chassis O6614946 was one of 25 similar buses with Weymann 52-seat metal-framed bodywork placed in service in 1937. On the left of the picture, behind an East Midland Leyland Tiger TS7 with Eastern Coach Works body of similar age, can be seen two Trent front-entrance double-deckers, also with Weymann front-entrance bodies but of composite construction — some of these were Regents and others on Daimler COG5 chassis. Just visible in the background, behind the ice-cream man's tricycle, is one of Barton Transport's newly-delivered Leyland Titan TD5 double-deckers with front-entrance Duple body. Behind the Barton single-deckers can be glimpsed a Nottingham Corporation trolleybus.

[Below] Another pocket of front-entrance double-decker territory at that period was around the river Tyne, although the vehicles were all owned by Northern General Transport Co Ltd or its subsidiaries. Tynemouth & District Transport Co Ltd, as it had become in 1934, took delivery in 1937 of three Regents with 7.7-litre engines and 52-seat Weymann bodywork of basically similar design to the Midland General vehicle shown above, though differing in numerous minor details — No. 95 [O6615287] is shown here photographed outside the 'goods inwards' entrance at Southall works. The absence of headlamps and reliance on fog lamps for normal driving — quite legal at that date — was quite common practice in parts of the North and Midlands, no doubt being chosen here partly as a means of dealing with the so-called sea fret often found on the North East coast. The vehicles were rebodied in 1949 with new Pickering rear-entrance bodies and sold in 1957 to the Gosport & Fareham Omnibus Company, where they operated until dismantled in 1964.

City of Oxford Motor Services Ltd tended to follow a traditional line, and this style of Park Royal 52-seat body on three Regents placed in service in 1937 was almost identical to those on a 1933 batch and, indeed, closely related to the original AEC-design lightweight body of 1931, although still acceptably contemporary in outline. The appearance was made more impressive by the Oxford fleet's distinctive red, maroon and duck-egg green livery. The chassis were standard 7.7-litre models with crash gearbox and, originally, indirect injection but within a few years they had been converted to direct injection. The vehicle shown, on chassis O6615290, was originally numbered K114, becoming KD114 following the engine modification and then H115 when the pre-war classification system was abandoned save for the prefixes H or L signifying 'highbridge' or 'lowbridge'. The whole batch was withdrawn in 1950 but sold to Northern General Transport Co Ltd, also a BET group company, which was short of vehicles at the time, thus becoming part of the same 'family' as the Tynemouth buses shown on the previous page which, by coincidence, had immediately preceding chassis numbers. The vehicle shown remained in NGT service until December 1954, saw brief further service with a London area independent operator and was scrapped a year later.

By 1937, the combination of Regent chassis and English Electric bodywork had become much less common than it had been in the early years of the model, despite AEC's association with this concern in regard to trolleybuses. However, Southend Corporation placed four examples in service with 53-seat lowbridge bodywork that year. English Electric had adopted a mildy curved front profile with a stepped cab front, but the sloping line of the top of the cab side windows was a feature continued from the previous generation of standard bodywork of this make. No. 210 [JN 9530], on chassis O6615299, was photographed in its later years, though substantially unaltered from original form.

Charles H. Roe had standardised on this curved-profile body design with the characteristic two-landing staircase from the end of 1936, beginning with a batch for Leeds City Transport consisting of 20 Regents and ten Leyland Titans, though several individual vehicles or batches with some related features had appeared earlier, the outline being derived from a body design for the side-engined AEC Q-type built in 1933 [see Best of British Buses No. 2, page 40]. Doncaster Corporation, a regular Roe customer but having no specific standard motor bus chassis preference, took delivery of two Regents with this body design in July 1937, No. 51 seen here being O6615284 — three single-deckers supplied at the same time were on Bristol JO5G chassis, a virtually unique double and single-deck combination though the Westcliff-on-Sea company favoured an opposite pairing at the time, with AEC Regal coaches and Bristol double-deckers. By this date it was usual for oil-engined double-deckers to be able to seat 56 passengers within the gross weight limit if the operator wished unless there was something unusual about the specification — these vehicles had the typical Roe seating split of 31 upstairs and 25 down.

Despite the Mansfield District Traction Co's close relationship to Midland General as a fellow member of the Balfour, Beatty group, conventional rear-entrance layout was chosen for ten Regents with Weymann metal-framed bodies purchased in 1937. The first two of these carried registration numbers VO 8589 and 8590 which had remained unused when the original 1932 order for Mansfield Regents had been cut back but No. 97 on chassis O6615428 was the first of the remainder which received contemporary DRR registrations. It is seen here in May 1953, still largely in original order apart from rubber-glazed destination indicators, and the loss of front wheel nut guard rings. The vehicle behind, Trent 1019 [RC 4625] was based on a slightly earlier chassis O6615064 but had received a new Willowbrook lowbridge body and later-type mudguards.

The first change to the Regent radiator since the production version introduced in 1929 was introduced in time to appear on the 1937 Show models. This photograph, taken outside the experimental department at Southall works in the Summer of 1937 shows a chassis fitted with a radiator having the new lengthened grille, extended downwards below dumb-iron level, probably as part of the re-styling process. The actual grille design, with narrow vertical slats, is of the type not introduced on production vehicles until late 1939. On the other hand the mudguard and front dash are of the type just about to be superseded by the style partially covering the front dumb-irons as shown overleaf. Note the electrical panel mounted to the right of the driver's seat, with switches, including the starter button, conveniently mounted along the top face.

Four changes considerably altered the appearance of the '1938 season' Regents, though each was interchangeable with earlier designs and no fundamental alteration in dimensions affecting bodywork were involved. The deeper radiator shell, as shown on an experimental installation illustrated on the previous page but retaining the close-woven wire-mesh type of grille, henceforth became standard. The modified front wing and dash panel were extended to form covers over the dumb-irons. Oil-engined chassis received a new bonnet design with no louvres. However, the most obvious change in side elevation was the adoption of a large chromium-plated hub-cap for the front wheels, replacing the wheel-nut guard ring and enclosing the hub itself. This was in line with the latest car styling and looked smart when in good condition, though prone to minor damage and, after a few years, peeling of the plated surface. This standard 7.7-litre example with Park Royal metal-framed lowbridge body was supplied to the Swan fleet of Swansea Bus Services Ltd. Seating capacity was 53, with 27 upstairs and 26 down, as was tending to become usual for a lowbridge bus. It makes an interesting comparison with the pioneer curved-profile Leyland-bodied Titan for this operator that had been built in March 1936 [see Best of British Buses No. 1, page 49] — the straight sloping front was by this date beginning to become dated, attractive though this vehicle looks in retrospect. No. 12 was on chassis O6615439.

Glasgow Corporation returned to the Regent clientele in 1937 after an absence of seven years with an order for 25 of the 100 double-deckers placed in service that year, the remainder of the order going to Leyland [50] and Daimler [25]. In 1938, however, there were 86 Regents and fifteen Albions, all but one having apt BUS registration numbers. No. 560 [BUS 126], on chassis O6616169, was one of 65 with Weymann bodywork of a general style, with curved profile but retaining the rounded projecting cab front, built by this coachbuilder mainly on Regent chassis for a number of operators at the time, though this version with characteristic destination display and mild 'streamline' livery style was special to Glasgow. The vehicle is seen when quite new, bound for the Empire Exhibition held in the city that year. Note the contemporary Leyland lorry, LMS railway horse-drawn delivery van and Corporation trams. Glasgow was one of a number of operators which continued to specify the earlier-style front mudguards in conjunction with the otherwise new-style front-end.

Despite AEC's replacement of the 8.8-litre oil engine by the 7.7-litre unit as the standard power unit for the Regent in 1935, the larger engine was not only alive and well three years later but being given a new lease of life by the introduction of the A180 direct injection version. Among early examples were four fitted in Regent chassis with preselective gearboxes for Dundee Corporation. They had Weymann bodywork of a new style with unbroken curved profile and — only just visible in this photograph — a new but significant styling detail in the downward sweep of the upper-deck cantrail mouldings at the front corner pillars. Note that the new style longer radiator, front wings and chromium hub caps were also applied to this version of the chassis — the 8.8-litre bonnet side now had no apertures, having never been given the access holes used with the smaller engines and now lacking louvres like the 7.7 version. No. 48 was registered YJ 5888 and had chassis O6615946.

Chapter Six: Regents à la carte.

By 1937-38, a curious situation had arisen in regard to Regent variations. Despite what no doubt seemed quite a healthy rate of output of over 1,000 vehicles per year, AEC was willing to produce the model in an almost bewildering number of variants to suit various customers. With hindsight, and particularly in the atmosphere of 45 years or so later, when the idea of departing from a standard model produces reactions of incredulity among manufacturers, one cannot help wondering if it was worthwhile.

However, quite a few variations were a simple matter of building in units which were fairly readily available. The 7.7-litre oil engine was standard and being built in sizeable numbers in both indirect and direct engine forms, while the 110 mm 7.4-litre petrol engine was still in production for coaches so could still be a standard option for Regents,

even though now fairly rare. Both preselective and standard 'crash' gearboxes were also available on tap, being produced in quantity.

The 8.8-litre oil engine was in a slightly different category. In addition to pressure from several municipal operators for its continued availability after officially becoming obsolete in 1935, London Transport was showing renewed interest. After the LT-type Renown conversions of 1934 when the petrol engines had gone into new STL chassis, no more 8.8-litre engines were purchased until 1937. But 24 more conversions were made that year, and a new version of the 8.8-litre engine was chosen for a new fleet of 266 Regal coaches for Green Line service. This was a direct-injection unit, using a combustion chamber and injectors of Leyland type, developed at London Transport instigation. This was also used for the

conversion in 1938-40 of most of the LT-type double-deckers dating from 1931 that were not already oil-engined, about 575 vehicles.

With this volume of interest, the 8.8's survival was assured and AEC also developed a toroidal-cavity direct-injection version — both versions were given the designation A180. What is more, it was this engine that was to be the basis of a new larger-capacity engine being developed to meet a fresh London Transport specification, which revealed that the 'big engine' school of thought, though temporarily in eclipse so far as production STL buses were concerned, was favoured for the future. This was the 9.6-litre, a swept volume achieved by increasing the 8.8-litre's bore size from 115 mm to 120 mm.

However, this change called for redesign of the bottom end, to give a heavier-duty crankshaft and

Neither of the six-cylinder engines visible on the production line at Southall in this June 1938 photograph were of the 7.7.-litre type which was the contemporary standard. Nearest the camera, an 8.8-litre unit nears completion, readily identifiable by its oil filler with horizontal filler cap on top of a cranked pipe [though the four-cylinder oil engines were similar in this respect]. Beyond is a petrol engine, still being built for a high proportion of Regal coach chassis sold to independent operators and hence available if an order for petrol Regents arose. Its oil filler neck was angled to bring the filler close to the access hole in the bonnet side — a similar arrangement was used for the 7.7.-litre oil engine.

bearing assembly and a half-way house was produced by marrying this to the existing 8.8-litre cylinder dimensions. This engine was designated A182, but the author has never come across firm evidence confirming that such a unit was ever fitted to an STL. However, AEC chassis records for the last three STL buses of the 1937-38 batch, O6615940-42 (STL 2513-5), show that they had engines recorded as of type A805/1, numbers 5, 6 and 7. The 'type number' looks more like an AEC experimental department or special order number, and it is known that these three buses had 8.8-litre experimental engines when new. They do not seem to have run long in this form, becoming indistinguishable from others of the type. This is in itself interesting, as an A165 or A180 installation would have required the usual 8.8-litre projecting radiator, requiring a slightly shorter than standard body to keep within the tight 26ft. length limit of those days, which would have made them require special identification. It is possible that the revised bottom-end allowed a more compact installation for, strange though it may seem, the 9.6-litre engine was fitted into much the same bonnet length as the 7.7 when it ultimately appeared in the RT-type bus, and the experimental 8.8-litre engines may have been the same.

Meanwhile work on the RT chassis itself, known at first by the experimental type number XU1631, had been put in hand in AEC's drawing office at Southall in 1937. This was almost completely new, from the frame upwards, and was to set the standard for the whole of what was later known as the Mark III range of passenger models. At first, however, it was intended entirely as a London Transport project, meeting that undertaking's aim at a bus which at the same time required less effort to drive, was more durable and gave higher standards of passenger comfort than the STL. The fluid flywheel and preselective gearbox were, of course, firmly established for a standard London bus, but the relatively heavy pedal action of existing spring operated preselective designs was to be overcome by using an air-pressure system. London Transport was by this date familiar with an air pressure operation of trolleybus brakes and this feature was also adopted, with a combined and, at the time, complex-seeming air system for both functions.

The 9.6-litre engine was not chosen to increase engine power and the nominal output of the original design, 100 bhp, was significantly down on that available from the indirect-injection 7.7.-litre unit, 115 bhp. But the larger engine gave much

better low-speed performance and the promise of both economy and, especially, longer engine life. The combustion system used was again the pot-cavity piston, following Leyland practice, and with a flexible engine mounting, a new feature for a Regent (though by then in regular use by Daimler and Dennis), the passenger was given greater refinement of running, if still not quite up to the smoother petrol-engine standards.

The first chassis was taking shape in Spring 1938. Meanwhile quite a variety of Regents were emerging from Southall. It is instructive to note the specifications as built of a sample of 61 buses which numerically followed after the 500 London STL-type chassis of 1937-38 of which the three 8.8-litre experimental buses were the last (see foot of page).

There were thus five different types of engine and eight different combinations of engine and gearbox in ten orders. Some of the Dundee buses were recorded as having been built with A165 Ricardo-head engines but it is thought that they may have been changed at an early stage — perhaps before delivery. The two demonstrators were both sold to Provincial (Gosport & Fareham) concern after a few months, by which time both had 7.7-litre engines — it is not known whether

This table shows the remarkable variety of engine and gearbox combinations represented in ten orders covering a total of 61 buses with consecutive chassis numbers built in 1938. See the third column of the text above for more detailed comment.

Chassis number	Operator	Engine type	Gearbox type	Registration numbers
O6615943-6	Dundee	A180 8.8 DI	D132 Preselective	YJ 5887 etc
O6615947-56	Cardiff	A173 7.7 DI	D132 Preselective	BBO 72 etc
O6615957-61	Aberdeen	A180 8.8 DI	D132 Preselective	RG 9803 etc
O6615962	Felix [Doncaster]	A173 7.7 DI	D124 Crash	CWY 758
O6615963	Demonstrator	A180 8.8 DI	D124 Crash	JML 784
O6615964	Demonstrator [Ribble]	A173 7.7 DI	D124 Crash	KMD 306
6615965	Douglas	A162 Petrol	D132 Preselective	DMN 850
O6615966-5995	Liverpool	A171 7.7 Ricardo	D132 Preselective	DKC 670 etc
6615996-6007	Northern Ireland RTB	A162 Petrol	D124 Crash	FZ 233 etc
O661G6008-13	Huddersfield	Gardner 6LW	D132 Preselective	BCX 236 etc

This vehicle was completed for use as a demonstrator to Bradford Corporation towards the end of 1938, in itself somewhat surprising as batches of Regents with 7.7-litre and 8.8 engines were already in service. The chassis number, O6615413, suggests that it had been built or at least ordered around the end of 1937, but the fleet number just visible on the front of the cab, 466, follows Bradford's 1938 batch of Daimler COG6 buses and the registration number, not yet applied in this picture, was JML 409 tying in with a late 1938 period. Weymann built the 56-seat body to its latest outline but with Bradford-style details, as on some of the Daimlers. At first glance, the appearance suggests a standard 7.7-litre chassis but a curious detail is the absence of the starting handle shaft which normally projected through the radiator by a couple of inches or so, even though a handle was only fitted to oil-engined models if specifically requested. Moreover there was no hole for it in the grille. It seems possible that there was something unusual about the engine installation and a logical possibility is that the engine was flexibly mounted [as standard on Daimlers at the time]. The vehicle, which had preselective transmission, as usual for the operator, was not acquired by Bradford Corporation until 1941 being withdrawn ten years later, retaining the radiator details as shown into the post-war period.

JML 784 (O6615963) was 'aimed' at any particular operator in its original form, but it is significant that a A180-powered bus was built as a demonstrator at all, for AEC never publicised such a model!

Also unpublicised, though more understandably so from AEC's viewpoint, were the Gardner-engined models built for Huddersfield. This municipal undertaking (which also looked after an equal number of railway-owned buses in a manner characteristic of parts of Yorkshire) had gained early experience of the Gardner 6LW six-cylinder engine giving 102 bhp from 8.4-litres in two Karrier single-deckers in 1932. Although AEC chassis had become standard after Karrier, in those days a Huddersfield firm, faded out of the motor bus business in 1933, and AEC oil engines were also tried, the Gardner units had obviously made a favourable impression. So AEC was persuaded to produce Regal chassis with 6LW engines from 1935 and, from 1937, Regents with this unit

also. The engine installation was copied from that on eleven LGOC Renown six-wheelers dating from 1932, with an even more pronounced forward projection of the radiator than required for the 8.8. Huddersfield already standardised on fluid flywheels and preselective gearboxes for its AEC buses and this feature continued, so in essence, the undertaking's 6LW-powered Regents were an AEC equivalent to the Daimler COG6 using the same engine and similar transmission, a good example of municipal determination to purchase the precise specification of bus desired and, equally, AEC's willingness to indulge such a preference, presumably arguing that it was better to sell chassis than nothing. There were six Regents in 1937, six in 1938 and four in 1939, all with O661G prefix to the chassis numbers 5316-21, 6008-13 and 6022-5.

Other notable instances of efforts to meet an operator's specifications concerned Birmingham. Clearly the loss of the 'second city's' bus orders

after 1931 exercised AEC's sales and engineering staff, understandably, as this was Britain's largest municipal fleet. From 1934, the Daimler COG5 chassis was standard, no doubt partly on the basis that the chassis was built within the county of Warwickshire and partly on the merits of the model, notably efficiency of the Gardner engine, of the five-cylinder 5LW-type in this case. Birmingham is not, on the whole, a very hilly city and 85 bhp was evidently judged enough.

AEC sold one batch of five Regents to Birmingham City Transport in 1937. They were relatively standard in basic type, with 7.7-litre engines and preselective gearboxes, though some trouble was taken in meeting Birmingham's more detailed requirements. Most notable was the adoption of the Daimler-style preselector quadrant control on the steering column rather than AEC's floor-mounted lever that looked like a conventional gear lever. They also had chromium-plated radiators

Huddersfield Corporation persuaded AEC to build Regent chassis with Gardner 6LW engines, thus acquiring vehicles with even longer bonnets than those with 8.8-litre engines. The Gardner unit was slightly longer despite its smaller capacity of 8.4-litres, but AEC's installation was, in any case, not particularly good in minimising the extra length — a neater job was done by some operators in subsequent conversions. However, the overall result was an impressive and, doubtless, efficient bus; with pre-selective transmission, the overall effect was not unlike a Daimler COG6 in terms of performance and sound effects. They had Park Royal 54-seat bodywork to a bow-fronted design sold also to neighbouring Halifax on the 8.8 chassis — this one, No. 137 [BCX 237] on chassis O661G6009, was one of six delivered in June 1938, of which three including this one had bodies of composite construction.

instead of the standard aluminium.

However, the first chassis of the batch O6615090-4 was earmarked for a curious experiment. It was fitted with a four-cylinder oil engine of type A168, the type used on the Regal 4 single-decker, preselective gearbox and 'borrowed' the Short Bros body from a 1931 Birmingham Regent temporarily taken out of service, retaining its number 483 and even receiving a matching registration number DOB 483 in typical BCT fashion. The chassis was returned to AEC, rebuilt with 7.7 engine and crash gearbox and sold to Provincial a few months later with a new Park Royal body and re-registered DAA 848. Thus, temporarily at least, the Regent 4 concept of the early 'thirties came into being. Apparently by coincidence, Provincial fitted two 1931 ex-Oxford petrol Regents with four-cylinder oil engines in 1940, these three being the only four-cylinder Regents, so far as the author is aware. Another 7.7-litre chassis, O6615149, was built to Birmingham specification to make up the original order.

Another Regent that might have been was the 'Regent Mark II' model O861 also planned as a venture with Birmingham in mind. This type number had been left blank when the Regal Mark II lightweight model with '6.6-litre' (actually 6.75-litre) engine had been introduced at the 1935 Olympia Show (see 'Best of British Buses No. 6'). Whether it had then been intended to introduce such a model is an intriguing question — the choice of O862 for the Regal Mark II as the model number may have simply been intended to match

up with the use of numbers ending in . . 2 for the standard Regal, O662, and four-cylinder version, O642. The performance would certainly have matched up to that of a COG5, but the economy would not, while the 6.6 was by no means AEC's best engine, so it was probably as well that the idea was not pursued.

Sooner or later the idea of a 5LW-engined model was bound to come up and doubtless the management of the Hull municipal undertaking were well aware of Huddersfield's AEC-Gardner buses. There was only one batch of 20 buses, O661G6544-63, built in 1939, though there were ultimately numerous conversions of petrol Regents with 5LW engines carried out by operators, particularly in companies under Tilling management. Hull did actually announce an order placed during the war for post-war delivery of a further batch of similar buses but these eventually materialised as 9.6-litre Regent III models — a very different animal.

However, these were the wilder fringes of Regent production in the final couple of years before the outbreak of war disrupted production. The chassis number sequence began to show sizeable gaps after about O6617083 due to cancelled orders — there were odd ones previously — so, in round figures, output of Regents entering service in 1938-9 and up to about the middle of 1940 was probably about 1,200. The outbreak of war in September 1939 undoubtedly cut production severely, so this might reasonably be regarded as equivalent to about two years output by normal standards. Even so, the rate was well down on earlier

levels, mainly due to a reduction in London Transport's intake after the big orders of the mid 'thirties, when STL buses had been entering service at an average rate of about 450 a year. After the end of the 500-vehicle STL2014-2513 batch in August 1938, only 283 Regents were built for London service in the period up to June 1940 (strictly speaking, the last 43 RT's were not bodied until 1941 and in one case 1942). Thus provincial sales at around 900 for the two years or so were well up on mid-'thirties level, and about three-quarters of these had the standard 7.7-litre engine, mostly in direct-injection form, which belatedly became officially standard in 1939.

About 200 of these had 8.8-litre engines of A180 or A165 types. Among the latter were some 67 in several batches for the Halifax fleet, then in process of a tram replacement programme. The General Manager of that undertaking, Mr G. F. Craven, was one of very few actively seeking more engine power and even the 130 bhp of the A165 engine did not satisfy him, in view of the hilly routes traversed. One of the 67, O6616351 (fleet number 64, registered JX 6897) was fitted when new in November 1938 with a Rootes-type supercharger, increasing the power output to 170 bhp, and making it easily the most powerful bus in Britain, a record not beaten until the late 'sixties. Four others, numbered 200-203 (JX 6939/6/7/8) with chassis O6616421/6338-9/6420, placed in service in April 1939, had their A165 engines converted to run on petrol with two Zenith carburetters and had the cylinder bore size increased to the 120 mm size giving the same swept volume of 9.6-litres as the new RT-type oil engine. The petrol version, probably derived from work on a military vehicle engine AEC was developing, had a reputed power output of 150 bhp, which seems slightly unimpressive by comparison with the standard 7.4-litre petrol engine's 120 bhp on one carburetter but was also enough to give them plenty of 'get up and go', particularly bearing in mind the contemporary unladen weight of about 6¾ tons. Fuel consumption was about 3½ mpg, not all that much worse than the fairly typical 4 mpg of a standard petrol Regent in urban service, but enough to cause Halifax to favour the supercharged oil engine which could manage to go nearly twice as far on a gallon of cheaper fuel. Unfortunately both experiments were brought to an end by the war and all five buses converted to standard.

About 21 other petrol Regents were built during this period, including another one for Douglas and five for Eastbourne Corporation in 1938 in addition to those tabulated. The latter were probably the last petrol Regent buses with standard A162 engine to be built. London Transport took

delivery of two petrol Regents fitted with lorry bodywork in 1939 but these probably had engines from LT's 'float' of spare units from conversions to oil, which amounted to hundreds by that date.

London Transport's intake of 283 Regents were allocated to chassis numbers O6616617-6899. The first 132 of these, entering service in the summer of 1939, were a final production batch of STL buses, basically similar to those built previously in having 7.7-litre engines, fluid transmission and 56-seat body built by LT at Chiswick. However, they had direct-injection engines from new and these were flexibly mounted and as a result pleasantly quiet-running internally, it evidently being considered by LT that the A173 was unacceptably harsh on its standard mounting (conversions to oil, using the same engine, of most of the sloping-front STL buses of 1933-34 which had fluid transmission carried out in 1939 also had flexible mountings, despite the considerable modifications this entailed). Outwardly the bodywork on the new buses, STL2516-2647, was very similar to the 1936-38 type, but they originally had the longer radiators of similar

outline to those used on provincial Regents from mid-1937 but not hitherto used on an STL.

The balance of the London Transport intake was even more interesting, being the RT prototype and the batch of 150 vehicles which constituted the first production RT order. The first chassis thus had the inconspicuous sounding chassis number O6616749 and it was decided to place it in service with an old open-staircase body from an ex-independent Leyland Titan, using the deliberately misleading fleet number ST1140. It was completed in this form in July 1938, and registered as EYK 396. It was withdrawn in January 1939 and the impressive new body intended for it was mounted, the vehicle thus reappearing as RT1 in April 1939, though several months passed before it entered service. Numerous detail changes were made to the chassis design before the 150 production vehicles were put in hand and RT2-151 did not begin to enter service until November 1939, by which time the outbreak of war on 3rd September had completely altered the outlook of the bus industry as well as the nation as a whole.

Export markets for Regents in the late 'thirties were mainly in Australia or South Africa. Here examples in the fleet operated by the Department of Road Transport, New South Wales, in the Sydney area are seen, in company with a Leyland Titan partly visible behind the vehicle on the right. The 7.7-litre Regent chassis followed the same pattern as standard models for home-market operators, the vehicle on the left having the short radiator and wings of 1937 or earlier style, while that on the right is from a later batch. The characteristically Australian style of bodywork, with strongly raked profile and high-waisted cab, were locally built mainly by two concerns, Waddington and Wood. Note the Vauxhall car, probably a Ten of 1938-39, with Australian-built tourer bodywork.

Morecambe Corporation remained faithful to the petrol-engined Regent throughout the 'thirties, building up a fleet of 38 by 1938. From 1936, Park Royal metal-framed bodywork was standardised as was the folding roof, which had become even more of a rarity on a double-decker by this date than earlier in the 'thirties when several operators had tried the idea. The largest and last batch of vehicles was one of ten delivered in 1938, No. 49, on chassis 6616078 subsequently registered DTB 48, being seen here. The chassis specification conformed to 1938 standards, with chromium hub caps, long radiator and the extended front wing shape. However, petrol-engined models retained the louvred bonnet and had a starting handle. Note that the external Autovac fuel-lift device was fitted on the dash behind the front mudguard — it had generally vanished on oil-engined models by that date.

Slightly later, and believed to be the last petrol Regents delivered as buses, were six for Eastbourne Corporation — several seaside resorts continued to specify petrol-engined chassis for their buses on grounds of the quieter operation. They had 48-seat bodywork by Northern Counties Motor & Engineering Co Ltd to that concern's unmistakable style of the late 'thirties, with upper-deck front dome almost indistinguishable from that at the rear, and rounded ends to the lower-deck side window. Similar bodywork had been fitted to Regents for other operators, notably Cardiff. This photograph of the last vehicle of the batch, No. 10 (JK 7431) on chassis 6616132, was taken in post-war days. Vision from the upper-deck front corner seats was not a strong point. A Standard Vanguard in van form, uncommon even when relatively new, can be seen in the background.

East Lancashire Coachbuilders Ltd of Black-burn was just beginning to make its name as a bodybuilder specialising in municipal buses in 1938. As was often the case in such circumstances, its early designs tended to be rather plain and the vehicle shown, Chester Corporation's No. 29 [DFM 390], on 7.7-litre preselective chassis number O6616297, did not have the attractive outline produced by this bodybuilder a year or two later. It was one of a pair of vehicles for this fleet, which favoured Massey Bros of Wigan for its 1939 order for four vehicles.

Nottingham City Transport took a somewhat utilitarian view of bus chassis appearance in 1938 when 20 Regents with 7.7-litre direct-injection engines, preselective transmission and Metro-Cammell 54-seat [28 up, 26 down] bodywork were supplied. The chassis had the pre-1937 short radiator [evidently to accommodate a radiator blind below] and 'plain' mudguards, while the front offside wheel had a step ring to aid driver access to the cab rather like the style used four years later on wartime Guy models. The bodywork was generally similar to the Metro-Cammell standard as built on Regent or Titan chassis for several municipalities, but with a number of special features such as the single-panel windscreen and radiused window corners. No. 4 [ETO 488] on chassis O6616247 is nearest the camera in this view taken at the body-builders, with Nos. 3, 2, 1 and 5 beyond. At the end of the line are two Daimler COG5 buses then being completed for Newcastle Corporation and having an equally distinctive body design variation of a slightly different general style Metro-Cammell tended to favour for Daimler chassis.

Halifax Corporation was not alone in continuing to favour the A165 indirect-injection Ricardo-head version of the 8.8-litre, which tended to be chosen by operators in hilly districts. No. 74 [JX 6930], on chassis O6616336, seen at Southall before application of the Halifax crest, was one of a batch of 25 chassis placed in service in 1938-39, mostly with preselective gearboxes and with bodywork by Park Royal, Roe or Weymann. In this case the body was by Park Royal and of composite construction, with the well-rounded curved-profile body styling which was virtually exclusive to Park Royal bodies for the Halifax and Huddersfield fleets. Unladen weight was kept down to 6 tons 13¾ cwt, allowing seating to be provided for 56 passengers. Four similar buses, including two from the same batch of chassis, which were placed in service in April 1939 were at first fitted with a special conversion of their A165 engines to 9.6-litre twin-carburettor petrol units, increasing the power output to 150 bhp for a particularly hilly route. Inevitably fuel consumption was heavy and when wartime fuel shortages dictated a search for economy the experiment was discontinued, but they must have been fascinating buses to ride in or drive.

Mr G. F. Craven, the Halifax General Manager, had also carried out a quite different experiment aimed at increasing power output. Another 8.8-litre Regent, chassis O6616351, Halifax No. 64 [JX 6897] with Roe 56-seat body, entered service in November 1938 fitted with a Centric supercharger increasing the power output from 130 bhp to 170 bhp. This made it easily the most powerful bus in Britain, a record that remained valid for many years after it was converted back to standard in 1940. Like the petrol versions mentioned above, it was a victim of the wartime need to conserve fuel, although it was stated in an article in 'AEC Gazette' in August 1939, from which this picture is reproduced, that consumption was only increased from 8 mpg to 7.3 mpg, neither of which seem unreasonable, even allowing for the modest weight by modern standard.

The supercharger was mounted under the floor, near the front of the lower saloon, and driven by belts from the propeller shaft connecting the engine to the preselective gearbox. It created air pressure of 5lb per square inch, fed into the engine intake manifold. 'Commercial Motor' reported that on a 1 in 6½ climb the speed was 15 mph "with the throttle barely half open". This was presumably unladen, but the fully laden power to weight ratio of about 16 bhp per ton implies that a modern double-decker running at 15 tons gross would need a 240 bhp engine to give similar performance. In other words, if it could be re-created, No. 64 could leave any standard modern double-decker standing on hilly terrain — such is progress!

Early in 1939, Brighton Corporation replaced its trams with a fleet of 44 trolleybuses and 21 buses, all AEC double-deckers with Weymann bodywork, painted and lettered in the style of the Brighton Hove & District concern which had taken over the former Tilling operations in the area. The buses were Regents with A180 8.8-litre direct-injection engines and preselective transmission. The engines incorporated the pot cavity combustion chamber system and so the buses had many of the characteristics of the contemporary 10T10 type of Green Line coach, with particularly smooth running and a distinctive exhaust note at times having a faint whistle-like characteristic. The Weymann bodies were of that concern's characteristic style of the period, with curved profile and radiused corner windows, and all looked virtually identical. They had seats for 54 passengers, with 28 on the top deck, though the first eleven were metal-framed, including No. 65 [FUF 65] on chassis O6616437 shown above nearest the camera, together with numbers 63 and 61, when about to be delivered from Southall. A Weymann official photograph of the same bus shows that it then had the traditional AEC-type of front wheel nut guard ring but this was evidently changed before delivery to Brighton in March 1939. No. 63, the next bus in line, was the one that was preserved after withdrawal, as shown on the front cover. On the right, No. 76 is seen when newly in service, passing the entrance to Brighton Aquarium, a scene that has altered little except that there is now a roundabout at this point. This bus, along with the other composite-bodied buses, was withdrawn in 1952, after a not unreasonable life of thirteen years but most of the metal-framed ones went on to some 24 years.

This is an extract showing the Regent models included on the wall chart used in AEC's drawing office as a key to the parts lists [not all shown here] for the versions counted as production standard types in 1939. It differed from the 'outside' publicity, which quoted only one Regent model, the 7.7-litre version, it being stated simply that "various additions and alternatives" to standard were available. Note that versions of the 7.7-litre model with fluid [ie preselective] transmission were available with standard 'solid' or rubber-mounted engines, the latter being equivalent to the final pre-war 15STL16 version of STL then being built for London Transport [though the special LT features were listed

elsewhere]. 'Regent A' was the 8.8-litre version, now with A180 direct-injection engine as standard [direct-injection was also now standard on 7.7-litre models, using the A173 engine]. 'Regent B' was evidently intended to be a double-deck equivalent of the special Regal single-deck chassis with shortened bonnet built for the Northern General and Scottish Motor Traction companies [see 'Best of British Buses No. 6', page 64] — it is not thought that any such Regents were built, but they would have been an answer to the Daimler COG5/60 model of similarly compact front-end design built for Coventry. Note that the RT-type is not quoted, being regarded as a London Transport 'special' at the time.

UNIT CHART 1939 PASSENGER MODELS.

NAME	MODEL Nº	WHEEL BASE	ENGINE				TRANSMISSION	LIST	UNITS																
			OIL OR PETROL	Nº OF CYLS	BORE x STROKE				ENGINE	PEDAL GEAR	GEAR BOX	EPICYCLIC GEAR BOX	CHANGE SPEED	MID AXLE	REAR AXLE	BRAKE GEAR	CLUTCH	FLUID FLYWHEEL	CARDAN FRONT	CARDAN REAR	INTER AXLE	FRONT AXLE	STEERING	RADIATOR
REGENT	O661/19	16'-3"	OIL	6	105 x 146 (7.7 LITRES)	STANDARD	BASIC STANDARD	A173	C147	D124	—	E122		F184	G218	J138	—	K147	K244	—	L139	M134	N164
						FLUID (S MOUNTED)	SV 53	SV53	SV53	—	D132	SV53		F184	SV53		J150	SV53	SV53	—	L139	M134	N164
						FLUID (R MOUNTED)	SV 108	SV108	SV108	—	D132	SV108		F184	SV108		J150 SV108	SV108	SV108	—	L139	M134	SV108
REGENT 'A'	O661/19	16'-3"	OIL	6	115 x 142 (8.8 LITRES)	STANDARD	SV 58	A180	SV58	D124	—	SV58		F184	SV58	SV58	—	K147	K244	—	L139	M134	SV58
						FLUID	SV 60	A180 6V60	SV60	—	D132	SV60		F184	SV60		J150	SV60	SV60	—	L139	M134	SV60
REGENT 'B'	O661/19	16'-3"	OIL	6	105 x 146	STANDARD	SV 97	A173	SV97	D124	—	SV97		F184	SV97	J138	—	K147	K244	—	L139	SV97	SV97
REGENT	661/19	16'-3"	PETROL	6	110 x 130 (7.4 LITRES)	STANDARD	SV 55	A162 SV 55	C147	D124	—	E122		F184	SV55	SV55	—	K147	SV55	—	L139	M134	SV55
						FLUID	SV 77	A162 SV 77	SV77	—	D132B	SV77		F184	SV77		J150	SV77	SV77	—	L139	M134	SV77

The prototype for London Transport's new generation of double-decker using the newly developed 9.6-litre oil engine had been under construction since early in 1938. The chassis was actually completed by AEC in June of that year and it was decided to fit it with old-fashioned looking Dodson open-staircase bodywork from an early Leyland Titan formerly owned by a London independent operator and place it in service to obtain experience of the chassis behaviour before the new body being built for it was ready. It seems clear that the intention was to persuade anyone who happened to see it that this was an old bus and the choice of fleet number, ST1140, can only be described as deliberately misleading, since the new model was slightly longer in wheelbase at 16ft. 4in. than the STL and in no way comparable to the ST. It entered service only briefly towards the end of the year from Hanwell garage [later renamed Southall], conveniently near to the AEC works and the usual home for experimental buses. It was then taken out of service and prepared for the new body, doubtless undergoing development of its many special features and in particular the air pressure system used to operate both brakes and the preselective gearbox. The photograph above was taken

at Southall in March 1939 just before the chassis, numbered O6616749, went back to Chiswick to blossom out with new body as RT1. Prominent in this view are the low radiator position designed to give minimum obstruction to driver vision, the steering column gear selector, echoing the latest American car practice [though much more suitable for such a location than a synchromesh control] and part of the complex-seeming air system on the chassis side.

The side view [below] of the LPTB-built body for RT1 shows that the classic outline that was to be so familiar to succeeding generations of Londoners was 'right' at the first attempt and needed only detail revision for succeeding versions built up to 1953. Traces of the STL were evident in the reverse curve at the rear end of the front mudguard and the staircase window intended for use by the conductor, but both of these were dropped later. The unladen weight of 6 tons 15¾ cwt was just above that allowing 56 seats within the 10½ ton limit, so this bus was a 55-seater, with 29 on top. It was completed in April 1939 but was subject to modifications of livery before being displayed to guests and the technical press in the form shown in July 1939. A new era had begun.

Contemporary deliveries of provincial Regents may not have been as exciting as RT1, but the general standard of body styling was reaching a peak which was not to be surpassed until some years after the war, already being seen as an ominous possibility. Colchester Corporation began a lengthy period of association with Massey Bros of Wigan when five Regents with 52-seat bodies of this make were placed in service early in 1939. Massey had begun to develop a distinctive if slightly flamboyant style, though it was not yet fully evolved. Nos. 30 and 33 [GVW 946 and 949] were on chassis O6616369 and 6372, being, like the rest of the batch, standard chassis with 7.7-litre engines and crash gearboxes. By now wheel nut guard rings were coming back in favour.

Glasgow Corporation's 1939 intake consisted of 25 7.7-litre Regents and 25 Albion Venturer double-deckers plus seven Albion single-deckers. Of the Regents, fifteen had Weymann 56-seat bodywork to a design basically similar to the 1938 batch but with a simplified version of the traditional Glasgow orange, green and cream livery. This profile, with projecting cab front, was beginning to look a little dated, though Glasgow was to revert to an even more traditional design in the early post-war period. Towing eyes were provided at the front of the frame and these prevented the use of the current standard mudguards covering the dumb-irons. However, Glasgow favoured the chromium hub cap. Note the fashionable outswept skirt on both designs on this page.

Chesterfield Corporation took delivery in 1939 of five Regents with 7.7-litre engines, fluid transmission and lowbridge bodies built by Metro-Cammell to a design which, though characteristically angular in overall outline, had a touch of Weymann practice in the styling treatment of the front dome. They seated 52 [26 on each deck]. Though not strictly a wartime bus, No. 45 [GNU 454] on chassis O6616528 typifies the situation just after the outbreak of war, with almost new vehicles bearing the first evidence of wartime austerity in the masked lighting [in this case relying on one foglamp, use of the other one being forbidden] and the early attempt at a means of preventing the interior illumination from being visible from enemy aircraft. The expressions on the pedestrians' faces mostly look rather careworn, though perhaps more due to the practical problems of the war than to bad news.

Chapter Seven: Wartime Regents.

The effects of the 1939-45 war preceded the actual event so far as Southall works was concerned, just as with many other parts of the motor industry. Big contracts for military vehicles or units for them had been placed as a consequence of the threat of war that had occurred during 1938 and, from about the Spring of 1939, bus orders were beginning to be delayed as these started to come through. The drop in output for London Transport was at least partly due to other causes, but probably came as a relief to the production control department already under pressure to get orders for Matador and other military vehicles out.

The order for the first production batch of 150 RT-type chassis for London Transport had been placed in July 1938 but not announced at that date as the new model was then a closely guarded secret. Manufacture of these did not begin until the summer of 1939, there being some delays due to such factors as the need for production to be set up of the air compressor at Clayton Dewandre, RT1's chassis originally having a German-made Bosch unit.

Meanwhile a second RT order, for 188 vehicles had been agreed in November 1938. AEC did make a public announcement about this one, though not until the August 1939

issue of 'AEC Gazette' which also included an illustrated description of RT1. In fact these vehicles were never built, and delivery of the 150 chassis that were completed was spread between October 1939 and May 1940.

Orders for provincial Regents were also still being completed during the early months of the war and the vehicles produced incorporated their operators' usual features. However, bodybuilding was often delayed and although some fleets received sizeable numbers of vehicles up to the fateful Summer of 1940 many of these were on chassis that had left Southall before the end of 1939.

Early wartime buses showed no sign of the restrictions on design or finish that applied later. This view of one of the author's favourite batches of Regents was taken in March 1940, when Charles H. Roe Ltd was completing an order for 20 examples for Leeds City Transport of which delivery had begun in December 1939. Wartime headlamp masks and white edging had not yet been applied to No. 123 [HUM 418] on chassis O6616928. Like most of Leeds' earlier Regents, these were 7.7-litre preselective buses and had Roe 56-seat bodywork — with this batch, there was a total of 100 examples with this basic body style with curved front-end, incorporating the Roe patented stairs and 31 up, 25 down seating. Somehow the Leeds engineers seemed to extract a crisper performance from their 7.7-litre engines, even when in the lowest-powered direct-injection form, than most operators managed. Roe had by this date adopted a windscreen with curved bottom edge for AEC chassis and the overall appearance in the original blue and cream livery was very attractive; this particular camera angle was perhaps the least flattering because of the abrupt step in the depth of the middle cream band at the corner of the windscreen. All 20 of the HUM-registered batch remained in service until 1956, five survived on driver-instruction until 1962-63 and one is now preserved.

Among the vehicles delivered in 1940 during this period were two that had been intended for the 1939 Earls Court Commercial Motor Show, cancelled due to the war. One was a Roe-bodied 7.7-litre Regent for Leeds, very like one exhibited at the 1937 Show, and the other was an RT-type chassis with Weymann body for Glasgow Corporation, the latter being the only RT sold outside London until after the war. However, mention should also be made of RT19 of the London batch, which was borrowed back by AEC in February 1940, when almost new, and used as a demonstrator until returned in August 1942.

After that, bodybuilding dwindled to a mere trickle, and bus chassis production to a standstill.

However, in 1941 it was decided that some supply of new buses would be essential and, as the first step, manufacturers were asked to assemble chassis for which they already had parts, these being nicknamed 'unfrozen' chassis, and AEC's contribution was 92 Regents. These had all the hallmarks of being manufactured as one production run, though the chassis numbers issued to them, O6617174-6/80/97-7201/07-

Though usually referred to as 'The pre-war RTs', none of the first production batch of RT-type buses were completed even as chassis until after the outbreak of war in September 1939. RT16 [FXT 191], on chassis O6616764, was one of the first seven to enter service, in January 1940, and was still in almost original condition and operating from the same garage [Chelverton Road] when photographed in August 1945. The Chiswick-built bodies differed only slightly in appearance from that on RT1, the most obvious changes being the simpler mudguard outline and the elimination of the staircase window. Somewhat surprisingly as it now seems in retrospect, the original livery was rather more complex than that on RT1, with the lower-deck window surround in off-white and silver-grey roof, the latter having changed to brown as a wartime measure. The downward curve of the lower-deck waist towards the offside windscreen pillar was perhaps the most obvious external difference between these buses and the post-war RT. Note that both upper and lower windscreen panels are slightly open; they were operated by a somewhat elaborate winding mechanism.

89, had several gaps, the intervening numbers never being used. They entered service between the Autumn of 1941 and the latter part of 1942. The specification for all these chassis as built was that of the 'plain' specification O661/19. The system of using suffix numbers to distinguish successive standard types had begun in the early days of the Regent, but meant little when operators had so wide a choice of alternative features. Originally the designation O661/19 could cover any oil-engined variation of those offered as production options in 1939, i.e. with 7.7-litre A173 or 8.8-litre A180 engine and crash or preselective transmission, and was thus of little value in identifying the precise variant of a particular vehicle.

However, the 'unfrozen' Regents were all fitted with A173 engines and crash gearboxes and were of virtually identical chassis specification. They

were allocated to nineteen operators by the Ministry of War Transport in a manner that suggested a bureaucratic rather than practical approach though it could be said that most recipients were already users of either AEC buses or engines. The bodywork included a remarkable variety of types. The largest allocation, of 34 chassis went to London Transport as STL2648-81, which no doubt seemed almost ideal, though the use of crash gearboxes had last been seen on a new STL in 1934. Of these, eighteen received what had been spare STL bodies of several types (including two with LGOC-built 60-seat bodies of the square-fronted 1933 type), and the remaining sixteen had new LPTB bodies to a design based on the standard STL but lacking some of the usual refinements. Some of the allocations to other operators received bodywork to peacetime design that was also in

the 'unfrozen' category, sometimes intended for an operator other than the actual recipient. Others were fitted with early examples of the so-called 'standard' body to the Ministry of Supply's wartime utility specification which had been introduced to simplify production. In fact, each bodybuilder produced its own design, the only features generally in common being the austerity of outline and such items as the reduced number of opening windows.

Thus it was that O6617289, a vehicle with Northern Coachbuilders body of this type allocated to Western Welsh was, for the time being, the last Regent. The quantity of vehicles built did not quite match up to the total implied by the last four figures of this number but, ultimately, post-war production was to more than double this impressive-seeming output. However, that story must wait for another volume.

Another of the first of the production RT buses, RT19 [O6616767] was borrowed back by AEC almost immediately after entering service for use as a demonstrator and toured the country, spending periods in service with potential customers. It is seen at Nottingham Corporation's Mapperley terminus on an unusually wet day in September 1940, the peak month of the Battle of Britain. By that date, lining out had been applied, presumably in an effort to make the London Transport red livery more 'municipal' in character, though somewhat out of character with the modern lines — later during its demonstration period, it was repainted light green. Note that no offside headlamp was fitted — although its use would have been forbidden at that period of the war, the lack of provision for an obvious future need was a curious omission, subsequently rectified. The chassis of this bus was later rebuilt to act as the prototype of the post-war 3RT-type chassis subsequently built in huge numbers and received the largely metal-framed body from RT1, re-entering service in this form in November 1945.

The only RT-type chassis to be delivered to an operator other than London Transport until after the 1939-45 war was Glasgow Corporation's No. 723, delivered in February 1940. It had been intended to be an exhibit at the Commercial Motor Show to have been held in London in the Autumn of 1939, but this event was cancelled. The chassis, O6616963, was almost identical to that of the London vehicles, but had the chromium-plated 1938-type hub caps which had been

abandoned as standard by that date but were still favoured by Glasgow. The Wey-mann bodywork was basically of contemporary standard Glasgow style but the flush-front cab gave a more modern-looking profile and may have been based on a London RT cab floor and bonnet assembly. The mudguards were of the Dunlop rubber type being used by a number of operators around that time, the front units being of the same outline as those on London's RT buses.

It remained in service until 1956 — Glasgow was to become a major operator of Regent Mk III buses of the type derived from the RT in the post-war years. It is not clear how AEC would have handled the sale of RT-type buses on the open market from 1940 had there not been a war, but it was clearly intended to do so from almost the beginning, unlike the belated Routemaster marketing exercise of the 'sixties.

Yet another Regent variant appeared in the early months of the war and although this photograph of O6616956 appeared in 'Blue Triangle' it is also included in this volume in the interests of comprehensive coverage. It seems possible that it, too, may have been intended as a 1939 Show exhibit but was in any case a 'one-off' vehicle, possibly a pre-production updated version of the 8.8-litre variant for operators unwilling to pursue the advanced specifications of the RT. It had the A182 engine and looks as if it may have incorporated a flexible engine mounting, judging by the lack of starting handle shaft. The radiator had the vertically-slatted grille, just on the point of being introduced as standard, and was mounted about 3in. further forward than with the 7.7, giving noticeably less of the protruding snout than the A165 or A180. The photograph shows Dundee Corporation No. 112 with wartime headlamp mask and the registration number YJ 7337. This was evidently surrendered or may have been an error, for the bus entered service as YJ 7586.

[Above] The Oxford company placed 20 Regents in service in 1940, and twelve of these, including D168 [JFC 792] on chassis O6617015, had Park Royal 54-seat composite bodywork with smoothly curved front-end profile, by then widely accepted as normal. The 7.7-litre [A173 engine] chassis had the vertically slatted radiator and the revived louvred bonnet and, apart from the pre-1937 style mudguards, was very much in line with the final O661-series Regents of 1941-42, and indeed 1946-48, in appearance. They were delivered in January 1940.

[Below] Placed in service slightly later, in May 1940, were ten Weymann-bodied rear-entrance Regents, also on basically standard 7.7-litre chassis with crash gearboxes, for the Northern General Group, but these had the 1938-39 type of bonnet without louvres and the wire-mesh radiator grille. They were well finished but may have suffered from the beginnings of a scarcity of light metals as the unladen weight at 7 tons 1¾ cwt, would have limited seating capacity a year earlier but 56 seats were permitted under relaxed wartime regulations. Two were supplied to the Tynemouth fleet, including No. 116 [FT 5226] on O6616941, remaining in service until 1956.

After a period of a year or so during which supplies of new buses had almost completely dried up as the war situation became more critical, authority was given by the Ministry of Supply to the completion of buses for which parts were in stock. AEC's contribution consisted of a total of 92 Regents, all built to the standard O661/19 specification, with A173 7.7-litre engines and crash gearbox. They were allocated by the Ministry of War Transport to some 20 operators, several of which had not operated Regents previously. Among them was Edinburgh Corporation, which took delivery of two, including G9 (DSF 983) on chassis O6617232 shown here, in November 1941. They had Park Royal 56-seat bodywork to the 'utility' specification which had just been put into effect to save man-hours, though Edinburgh had improved the appearance by painting them in its normal livery. A total of eight such vehicles was built, the Newcastle Corporation and Rhondda fleets receiving three each.

Many of the 'unfrozen' Regents, as they were called, received bodywork largely of peacetime standard, quite often intended for some other operator. Allocation of vehicles by the MoWT was sometimes surprising, as when Coventry Corporation, with a serious vehicle shortage caused by heavy bombing of that city, received only three of ten Brush bodies to its special 60-seat design while six went to Midland Red and one to Hull. Midland Red considered the rearward-facing seat for five passengers at the front of the lower saloon unsuitable and promptly had its examples re-arranged to seat 59, with 31 upstairs and 28 down, thus defeating the aim of saving manpower which lay behind the scheme. GHA 797, on chassis O6617213, is seen in service later in the war period, having become a little battered around the mudguards, as tended to happen in those days of blackout and limited repair facilities.

Understandably, London Transport received the largest single share of the 'unfrozen' Regents, 34 in all, or just over a third of those built. Although 34 new bodies were put in hand by LPTB Chiswick works, it was decided that eighteen of the chassis would receive existing overhauled bodies of earlier types from the float hitherto maintained to suit the LPTB overhaul procedure, in which bodies were removed and took longer to repair than the chassis from which they came — generally three spare bodies were produced for every 100 buses, though many had been used to repair air-raid damaged vehicles. Almost all types of STL were included among the eighteen and so two of the new chassis received 60-seat bodies of the type fitted to the first batch of STL buses. Thus STL2679, registered FXT 402, and on chassis O6617250, appeared on the road in January 1942 with a body built by LGOC about nine years earlier. The chassis did not carry the standard AEC mudguards, acquiring a set appropriate to the type of body, but the radiator and bonnet were of standard O661/19 style as on other 'unfrozen' chassis. The reversion to crash gearboxes implied a step back in time for LPTB and although the 34 buses thus produced were at first painted in central area red livery, they were sent on to country area routes and later repainted green. STL2679 is seen after withdrawal from public service when being used for staff transport between Hounslow garage and Aldenham, operating on an LPTB trade plate 081 GF.

The sixteen new bodies built at Chiswick in 1941-42 were basically to standard STL design and did not conform to the utility specification except that they were lacking in some of the normal equipment and had the style of seats used in pre-1936 series. The last fifteen had no separate front route number box, giving them an outline also rather like pre-1936 vehicles. STL2676 [FXT 399] was among the last to appear, entering service in August 1942, though seen here later in its career, soon after being repainted in the post-war green and cream livery, operating from Godstone garage on route 411.

End of the line. The Western Welsh Omnibus Co Ltd received four 'unfrozen' Regents, all having bodywork to wartime specification by Northern Coachbuilders Ltd of Newcastle-upon-Tyne, a bodybuilder little known outside its own area until wartime. Two were highbridge and two lowbridge. The latter, shown here, were of the 55-seat capacity and 27 upstairs, 28 down seating layout standard on wartime lowbridge buses. The vehicles, parked opposite NCB's then premises, were painted in unvarnished grey and had not been signwritten. They also lacked registration numbers and were probably to be delivered in this condition, as usual with utility buses. They were on chassis O6617284 and O6617289, the latter, No. 607 [CKG 291] being numerically the last new Regent until production was resumed at the end of the war.

This superb night photograph, the unmistakable work of Geoff Atkins, effectively captures the atmosphere of an early 'thirties Regent at work. The vehicle shown, on chassis 6612058, was one of two supplied to West Bridgford UDC in 1933 with 110 mm petrol engines, fluid flywheel transmission and Brush 56-seat bodywork. One can almost hear the gentle tickover of the engine and the murmuring of the Daimler-built preselective gearbox in neutral as the driver waits for the conductor's signal to leave the Nottingham terminus. Then, with the gear engaged and a brightening of the lights as the dynamo begins to charge, No. 23 would glide away with quite a soft exhaust note and the gearbox note changing in a glissando at each gear-change. The bus was about two years old when the picture was taken, in typically smart West Bridgford condition, though someone seems to have just caught that nearside front wing.

Chapter Eight: Pre-war Regents in retrospect.

History, and inherent durability, meant that few Regents had been scrapped when war broke out in 1939. When the model first appeared, in 1929, many bus operators' expectation of vehicle life was about seven years, and appreciably shorter careers were not unknown. By the late 'thirties, experience with both Leyland and AEC six-cylinder models in particular were causing that estimate to be extended. Even so,

a ten-year old Regent was generally regarded as due for retirement and London Transport intended to make a start on withdrawing its open-staircase examples in 1940. The idea of rebodying double-deckers had not caught on to the extent that applied to single-deckers.

But the outbreak of war effectively froze almost all ideas of withdrawal, particularly as AEC spare parts were still generally available (unlike

some other makes) and were to remain so for many years. One or two operators allowed some early Regents to go for scrap during the war years, but such action was so rare as to seem almost startlingly wasteful. The other side of the coin was the extensive rebodying and/or conversion from petrol, usually with A173 7.7-litre engines, though sometimes with Gardner 5LW units, that was carried on in many fleets from about 1942.

Several operators had fitted oil engines to some of their petrol-engined Regents but London Transport's conversion programme for some 286 examples dating from 1933-34 carried out in 1939 was extensive both in terms of numbers and the elaboration of the conversion itself. The vehicles in question had been built with fluid flywheels and preselective gearboxes and had 56-seat bodywork, thus conforming to the specification that had become standard for the STL class, apart from their petrol engines. London Transport was just changing over to the A173 direct-injection version of the 7.7-litre engine on the new STL buses built in 1939 which were unusual in having flexible engine mountings. Somewhat surprisingly it was decided to include the same type of mounting as well as engine for the conversions, instead of simply bolting the new engines in where the old ones came out. Not only did this imply considerable changes to the frame but the need to provide more clearance between the sump and the front axle made it necessary to put packing pieces under the front springs. This gave the converted vehicles their characteristic "begging dog" attitude — an apt phrase coined by the author's late colleague, E. J. Smith. Here STL289, one of the last of the type having the Daimler-built version of the preselective gearbox, waits in the sunshine at Kensal Rise terminus of route 6 in the late 'forties. The body on this particular bus had a minor unusual feature in the external ventilator at the front of the roof. These vehicles were appreciably quieter to ride in than the later standard STL buses, certainly after they were converted to direct-injection without alteration to the engine mounting, but forward vision for lower-deck passengers was poor and the interior finish somewhat austere.

Such conversions had begun before the outbreak of war, a notable example being that in 1939 concerning STL buses of London Transport dating from 1934 that had been fitted with petrol engines from LT-type Renowns. Another frequent occurrence was the conversion of indirect-injection Ricardo head engines to direct-injection — quite a major exercise, involving new cylinder heads, sets of pistons and other parts, but one reckoned especially worthwhile in wartime as a means of saving precious fuel. The bulk of the STL class was tackled in this way, beginning in wartime though the size of this job meant that it could not be completed until the early post-war period. The standard economy power setting used by London Transport and many other operators was 86 bhp, a figure which sounds very low by comparison with the 115 bhp of a 7.7 Ricardo engine at its full rating

but in fact still gave the relatively light STL, weighing only about 6 tons 12 cwt. unladen, quite a reasonable performance aided by the prompt gearchange possible with the preselective gearbox.

However, many early Regents were not modified in any major respect and yet it was quite common to find fleets that had survived until 1939-40 still largely intact until about 1948-50, thus virtually doubling even the longest original planned lives.

As supply of new vehicles caught up with demand operators began to withdraw vehicles slightly earlier. In London, the critical factor so far as STL-class buses were concerned was usually the body condition. In particular, the 1937 Park Royal bodies, of welded construction, had suffered structural corrosion to an extent not considered economically repairable by 1948 while, conversely, within the

big post-war programme of construction on new RT-type buses, it was looking as though there would be a chassis shortage. So it was decided to rebuild some STL chassis to RT dimensions to allow them to accept the new RT-type bodywork. The chassis first chosen were those built in 1939, perhaps because they already had one RT feature in their flexible engine mountings, the plan being to fit the 1939 bodies thus released, and still being mostly quite sound, on to 1937 chassis.

However, the major task was the rebuilding of the STL chassis to accept the RT bodywork, which took longer than anticipated. Although the engine, transmission, axles and vacuum brakes were unchanged, the frame had to be dismantled and the side-members heated to allow them to be reset to the RT-type shape, which did not have the inward taper over the front section. New RT-type radiator, steering and pedals were used. With the new standard bodywork they looked just like new RT buses. However, they immediately proved unpopular. The trouble was that they did not go or, more especially, stop like an RT.

In fact, the increase of unladen weight compared to the STL was only about 10 per cent, so performance was probably not much down, especially as fully laden this difference would diminish to about 6 per cent. But psychologically, they looked as though they should perform like a standard 9.6-litre RT, which they were incapable of doing. A total of 160 vehicles were converted during 1949 and all had gone by August 1954, lasting in the event no longer than the last unmodified STL buses. The chassis conversion was reputed to cost over £1,000 each, over half the cost of a completely new chassis at the time, so it was an expensive exercise. Fortunately the interchangeability of bodies meant that the 160 bodies could readily be transferred to new RT chassis. With hindsight, it might have been more cost-effective, and better pschology from the driver's viewpoint, to rebody a similar number of STL chassis in conventional fashion with new bodies to fit the existing chassis. Admittedly the bodies could not have been transferred to RT chassis when the vehicle supply position improved, but the vehicles would have been more readily saleable than the SRT chassis which no-one wanted by that date.

With occasional exceptions usually associated with sub-standard life of original bodywork, provincial Regents built in the 1934-40 period were not so often rebodied as had applied to some earlier batches. This was partly because many of them had good quality metal-framed or in some cases teak-framed bodywork which lasted quite well even when neglected during wartime. Also by the time decisions on possible extension of their life in this way arose, the need was often diminishing. Even so, some long life-spans were achieved, fifteen years or more being quite commonplace for whole batches and 18-23 years not unknown for individual vehicles, even with original bodies. New bodywork extended the life of several batches of vehicles in various fleets to around 20-24 years, but the clear leaders in terms of vehicle life were two buses of the famous Provincial (Gosport & Fareham) fleet, No. 35 which ran in service from 1936 to 1966 with original Park Royal bodywork, (apart from a switch of upper-deck with another similar vehicle after suffering damage in a low bridge accident), and No. 34, also with chassis dating from 1936 and which ran until 1970, having been rebodied in 1955.

The author, growing up in the days when the early Regents had their lives extended due to the 1939-45 war, almost began to believe they were immortal. Adolescent romanticism this may have been, but they could last ...... and last.

When Brighton Hove & District Omnibus Co Ltd fitted nine of its earliest Regents with new open-top bodywork built in its own workshops in 1936, it revived the idea of such vehicles, putting them in a new role as a seaside attraction. It is probably also true to say that they helped to foster the idea of fitting smart new bodywork on existing double-deckers, already becoming common practice with single-deckers. No. 6011 [GJ 2011] with chassis number 661565 had been placed in service by Thomas Tilling Ltd in the early Summer of 1930.

Conversely, the open-topped Regents taken over by London Transport in November 1933 with the business of C. H. Pickup [see page 35] were all rebuilt with covered tops within a year. The method used was to graft a new Chiswick-built top deck of the type used on new STL double-deckers at the time on to the existing Park Royal lower deck of the vehicles as built in 1932. This was doubtless the most economic way of achieving the desired result but it produced an odd effect from an appearance viewpoint as the lower deck had six bays between bulkheads and the upper-deck five over the same length. This may not have struck the Chiswick staff as unduly odd as there were still plenty of the NS double-deckers of the late 'twenties with a not dissimilar effect in service, and it has to be conceded that the resulting frontal appearance was not unattractive. The seating capacity was slightly reduced, with 27 on the new top deck and 26 below. GW 1785 on chassis 6611803 had been given the fleet number STL555 and is seen here in the late 'thirties — it had been rebuilt in September 1934 and ran in this form until 1948.

[Above, left] Bus manufacturing and operating engineers were already giving thought to alternative fuel supplies before the outbreak of war and almost immediately after this occurred in September 1939, London Transport fitted ST1100, on chassis 661163, one of the Regents dating from May 1930 and originally operated by East Surrey, with a Bellay gas producer mounted on an extension to the frame behind the rear platform. The photograph taken outside the AEC experimental department reveals that the Ransomes-built body was already showing signs of sagging of the framing to which timber-framed bodywork was often prone, even though still quite smart in the contemporary country area two-tone green livery. Permission had been given for such conversions to infringe normal regulations on length, etc but ground clearance and even the handling of the bus must have been adversely affected. ST1100 was converted to haul a separate producer-gas trailer within two months. In 1942-43, petrol Regents were often chosen for the producer gas conversions which were imposed on operators as a means of reducing fuel demand.

[Above right] Another early Bellay plant was fitted to Glasgow Corporation Regent 559, a 1938 Weymann-bodied bus [O6616168] which also returned to Southall in March 1940 for the purpose. However as diesel engines required some supply of their normal fuel to provide a means of ignition and the potential savings were less, such conversions were less common. This vehicle also operated with a trailer for a time.

[Below] Rebodying of early Regent chassis had occurred only on a very limited scale before the outbreak of war, but the shortage of new chassis soon evident led operators to such a policy. Among the earliest examples were two for the Gosport & Fareham [Provincial] fleet on 1931 chassis from the City of Oxford fleet. Chassis 6611116 [JO 1628] is seen here at Southall immediately after receiving new Park Royal bodywork of the style hitherto exclusive to the Halifax and Huddersfield fleets and, unusually, four-cylinder AEC oil engines. These vehicles received minor bomb damage in the AEC service station during an air raid and there is evidence of panel replacement in the photograph.

Air raids damaged enough of London Transport's buses in the Summer and Autumn of 1940 to cause a severe if temporary shortage of vehicles even though the majority were repairable. Some 473 buses were hired from operators based all over the country. They were of many different types, though a total of 124 Regents were included, no doubt being far less of a problem to maintenance staff than those of less familiar makes. The first to arrive came from Halifax, and that undertaking's No. 10 [JX 1788], O6612691, was the subject of some publicity photographs when operating on the famous route 11. It had been new in May 1934,

having 52-seat [later increased to 56-seat] Park Royal bodywork. Despite the basic familiarity of the model, this was an 8.8-litre Regent, a variant not normally found in central London. The hired buses returned to the provinces in 1941 and No. 10 resumed its normal duties in Halifax until sold to Nottingham Corporation in 1948, again helping to cover a shortage of buses but this time because of the post-war delays in delivery of new buses. The location, opposite the Grosvenor Hotel with part of Victoria Station in the background, is readily identifiable and it is a little surprising that it was passed for publication by wartime censors.

Slightly later in the war period, London Transport was able to return the favour and most of the ex-Tilling ST-type buses then operational and over 140 of the ex-LGOC version of the same type were hired to operators in various districts. ST512 [GH 3854], an ex-LGOC bus placed in service in September 1930, is seen while operating for Young's Bus Service of Paisley on one of that company's services into Glasgow during the period from August 1942 to June 1943 when it operated there. It returned to London and remained in service until December 1948.

Rebodying of early Regent chassis became quite commonplace during the war years, but the Eastern National and Southern National Omnibus Companies share the distinction of putting new bodywork on the oldest examples. Three of the four 'pre-production' vehicles built in the Spring and early Summer of 1929 originally placed in service by their predecessor, the National Omnibus & Transport Co Ltd, were so treated, and if ENOC could claim the oldest of these, 661002, SNOC had new bodies fitted on both of 661005 and 661007 in 1943. These were by Beadle, being built to that concern's characteristic style which was virtually unaltered from the late 'thirties to the late 'forties and largely unaffected by the wartime austerity period. This photograph taken in 1948 shows chassis 661005, Southern National No. 2905 [TK 3024] as running at that date. The Autovac fuel tap instructions refer to 'petrol' so evidently it was not re-engined up to that date, but may well have been later as it was not withdrawn until 1954, when the chassis was some 25 years old — not bad for a semi-experimental vehicle!

London Transport found itself short of lowbridge buses by 1942, having only the eight on ST-type chassis and the twelve 'Godstone' STL buses. So the final 20 of the 34 bodies built by the LPTB Chiswick works [and the last production batch of bodies built there] to balance the 34 'unfrozen' Regent chassis of 1941-42 were to a new design based on the familiar STL outline but of low-height layout with side gangway on the upper deck and some slight but noticeable variations in window levels. They also followed the Ministry of Supply 'utility' specification only in minor respects such as a reduced provision of opening windows and absence of any rear destination indicator, and were of the 27 up, 26 down seating layout which had been usual on late 'thirties lowbridge buses rather than the wartime 27/28. Externally they were distinguished by an unusual layout of between-decks moulding. None were fitted on the unfrozen chassis and they were mounted on various standard 7.7-litre oil-engined fluid transmission STL chassis with numbers between 1617 and 2311, dating from 1936 to 1938. One of the twelve red-painted ones allocated to Harrow Weald for route 230, STL2217 [O6615644], is shown above — note the stencil route number indicator in the lower-deck rear window. Below, the highest-numbered vehicle of this type. STL2311 [O6615738] is seen in rural surroundings at Biggin Hill, operating from Godstone on route 410 and smartly repainted in post-war country area livery.

Towards the end of the war period, a few operators placed experimental vehicles in service with the object of assessing possible new ideas for their post-war fleets. London Transport converted a series of vehicles to try out possible systems of fare payment immediately after boarding the bus, Continental style. The first was based on trolley-bus No. 61 and the second on a standard STL dating from 1937, which was rebuilt with a centre-entrance, cash desk for the conductor facing passengers as they boarded, and staircase ascending rearwards over the offside rear wheel arch. The total seating capacity was unchanged at 56, but there were 32 seats upstairs and 24 down. STL 1793 [on chassis O6614725] entered service in this form shortly before the war in Europe ended in 1945, on route 65 from Kingston garage. London buses were still being fitted with anti-blast netting on the side windows, with small diamond-shaped apertures to allow passengers to see out, because of the continued threat of enemy attack, by then largely from V2 rockets. Another similar vehicle, STL 2284, was converted with a more elaborate two-door layout in November 1945 but neither was a success, passengers disliking the pay as you board principle, then novel in Britain, and the vehicles were rebuilt back to standard.

In June 1945, with the end of the war in Europe, headlamp masks could be removed, but this Brighton Hove & District Regent was still in wartime grey paint and even the white patches on the mudguards had not yet been painted out. No. 6278 [GW 6278] on chassis 6611781 was otherwise looking very largely as built in 1932. The open staircase, already a feature generally regarded as obsolete even when this batch of buses was new, still remained, though not visible in this view due to its position slightly inset from the body side, and giving an odd short-tailed illusion to the appearance. However, like many other BH & D Regents, it would have sounded very different, having been fitted with a Gardner 5LW five-cylinder oil engine. It was subsequently sold to another Tilling group company, Hants & Dorset Motor Services Ltd.

The ex-Tilling Regents that were to remain in the Brighton Hove & District fleet were all greatly modernised in appearance by being fitted with new bodywork, a process that had begun in the late 'thirties but which accelerated as the war drew to an end, the largest group receiving this type of Eastern Coach Works 56-seat body, to a design closely related to that concern's immediate post-war highbridge standard. B H & D was allowed to depart from the standardised Tilling post-war colour schemes because of the agreement with Brighton Corporation and so these vehicles were in the characteristic Brighton style combining red with more extensive use of cream. No. 6261 [GW 6261] belonged to the same batch as the vehicle shown above, having chassis 6611764, but looked very different when photographed in July 1949. It also had a Gardner 5LW engine, as had over 50 B H & D Regents running in the late 'forties though there were also fifteen that had been converted with AEC 7.7-litre oil engines.

Yeoman's Motors of Canon Pyon, Herefordshire, operated a remarkable collection of AEC buses, largely built up during the 1939-45 war, although new Regal single-deckers had been purchased from 1929. Despite appearances, this was a Regent, chassis number 661748, built in 1930 and originally intended for the Birmingham Corporation fleet as one of a batch of 40 vehicles to be bodied by English Electric at Preston. The chassis was damaged in an accident when in course of delivery and replaced in 1931 by one of the early oil-engined chassis, O6611127, which took up the unused fleet number 408. Meanwhile 661748 was sent for repair to Oswald Tillotson and it was decided to body it as a single-decker, being sent to Burlingham at Blackpool [Tillotson's favoured bodybuilder] where it emerged in 1931 as a 32-seat coach. It was sold to S. H. Slack & Son of Middleton-by-Wirksworth, and registered as VU 5435. The coach was taken over by the North Western Road Car Co Ltd in 1932, becoming No. 207 in that fleet but sold to a dealer in January 1938. Yeoman's bought it in 1940 and it is seen running in the early post-war period, where it was sometimes to be seen in the company of another AEC more readily traceable to the Birmingham fleet, the prototype AEC Q AHX 63 [see Best of British Buses No. 2, page 89]. The body is thought to be basically the original so extensively modified as to be virtually unrecognisable. It remained in Yeoman's service until 1949, for the final year or so with the Radnorshire Motor Services section of the business.

Another Yeoman's body rebuild was that carried out on the Short Bros body of another Regent, dating from earlier in 1930. This was 661078 which had been one of five similar vehicles supplied to Chester Corporation, numbered 16 and registered FM 5776. Yeoman's bought it in 1942, but it had spent a brief period with Canvey & District Motor Services previously. In 1946 the body was completely rebuilt, retaining the six-bay layout of the original but being so extensively altered in appearance as to resemble a new body, vaguely reminiscent of wartime styles at the front but with radiused corners to almost all windows.

Former AEC demonstrators had been sent out in such numbers as to be represented in most parts of the country. Two which were a familiar sight to the author from his schooldays in the late 'thirties until he left the Newcastle area in 1948, are seen below. On the left is AML 664 on chassis O6612270, built in 1933 and having typical Park Royal bodywork of the period. After demonstration service it came into the fleet of County Motor Services of Stakeford near Choppington, Northumberland, a concern which had also added former Leyland and Daimler double-deck demonstrators to its fleet. All were acquired by United Automobile Services Ltd, which took over the business in three stages, and AML 664 was numbered AOH 1 ['AEC oil highbridge'], when purchased in June 1937, being the only Regent in the United fleet, though sizeable numbers of single-deck AEC vehicles were operated. By that time it had a 7.7-litre oil engine and seated 54 [28 up, 26 down]. It was allocated with one of the ex-County Daimlers to Whitley Bay depot, both

having Daimler-built preselective gearboxes, and regularly operated on route 17 to Newcastle, when it was photographed in 1947. The body had been rebuilt, but not much altered in appearance, by United.

On the right is EML 876, of basically similar specification but built in 1936, thus having an AEC-built preselective gearbox. Its 7.7-litre engine was an early direct-injection unit and the seating capacity was 56, with 30 upstairs. It arrived in Newcastle in grey primer and operated thus until November 1937 by which date it had been purchased and numbered 196, although sometimes nicknamed 'Emily' from the registration letters. Most records seem to quote the chassis number as O6613792 but the author's early notes, recorded from the vehicle, show O6613720 which according to other sources was another demonstrator, EML 154, purchased by Baker Bros of Warsop, suggesting that there may have been some administrative mix-up. It is seen in immediate post-war livery. Both vehicles were withdrawn in 1951.

In the post-1945 period, London Transport's ST-class buses were mostly showing their age somewhat, and the 'oddments' of interest to the enthusiast but presenting something of a maintenance problem to the operator might have been expected to the the first to vanish, but this was not always so.

The first of the type, ST1, registered UU 6614 and on chassis 661074, dating from December 1929, probably survived to about an average age for an LGOC-bodied ST because it was virtually standard particularly as the body finally fitted was a typical example of the class, built by LGOC and first operated on ST739 entering service in February 1931. It was photographed [above left] by the author near Holloway garage in December 1949, the same month it was withdrawn and sent for scrap — London Transport, despite its policy of preserving representative vehicles, did not make any fuss about the end of so historic a vehicle. This may thus be its last photograph, though that is a thought that only came to light in course of writing this caption.

Although the first, ST1 was not the oldest of the type, a distinction which belonged to the highest-numbered vehicle then in the class, ST1139, seen [above right] in Windsor in its final days. This vehicle, on chassis 661008, had been one of the pre-production batch and was originally placed in service by the East Surrey Traction Co Ltd [see page 15] after being registered as UU 6610 by the LGOC, thus belonging to the same registration batch as ST1. They went separate ways and this vehicle did not receive its fleet number until 1935 though also in the London Transport fleet from 1933. The original Short Bros open-staircase 51-seat

body had been slightly modified to accept a bigger destination indicator and the cab door had been replaced by a typical London-style opening. It was scrapped in October 1948, by which date the majority of the ex-Tilling open-staircase ST buses had already gone.

However, by far the most remarkable ST survivors were the eight lowbridge buses — six originally operated by National Omnibus and Transport Co Ltd at Watford [though on chassis and having fleet numbers from LGOC's first production batch] and two from the Amersham & District fleet. London Transport found itself very short of lowbridge buses during and after the war years, and these vehicles were given more extensive body overhauls than their highbridge contemporaries. Except for one of the Amersham buses, they all originally had Short Bros bodywork, but they were rebuilt at Chiswick works to varying degrees, mostly acquiring more of a characteristic LGOC-style appearance. ST140 [661348], originally dating from May 1930, was typical, with LGOC-style waistrail and rubbing strip in addition to the standard LGOC ST-type cab which did not quite line up with the rest of the body. The final touch was their conversion with 7.7-litre oil engines in 1949-50 — by that date London Transport had a ready supply of these from STL-type buses scrapped because of their body condition. ST140 seen here at Staines was one of the last five to operate, not being withdrawn until October 1952, and operating for two more years with independent operators. The Regal single-decker behind is also of interest, being T156, built for LGOC to replace T38 'borrowed' as a basis for the first Green Line coach.

London Transport decided to adopt a mainly red livery, with upper-deck window surrounds and a between-decks band in cream as its livery for the post-war RT-type fleet and also for the STL class after the war. Other pre-war types and the wartime buses on other chassis remained in the red and white that had been standard before the war, but without the black edging between colours and with the dreary red oxide roof that had originally been adopted in wartime in place of the 'silver' to make vehicles less conspicuous from the air. This 'class distinction' gave the STL-type buses a slight air of superiority and, indeed, the post-war livery suited them quite well.

However, the change of colour was by no means necessarily related to a major body overhaul. The backlog of work never carried out due to the war and the need to keep buses in service long after their intended withdrawal dates until the supply of new buses caught up meant that

only a limited number of STL buses were given full body overhauls restoring them to the standard that had been normal in 1939. The standard Chiswick-built ash-framed STL body had not been intended to last more than about ten years and even that was based on thorough and regular rectification of faults. STL 1762 [chassis number O6614964] dating from 1937 looked quite smart when photographed in the sunshine at the Kensal Rise terminus of route 6 about thirteen years later. But closer study reveals the external steel strapping that had been applied to the two pillars nearest the fuel filler. These were attached by coach bolts running right through the original pillars and incorporated cross pieces at waistrail level to hold the body structure together. Such methods had to be applied to many of these vehicles. This particular bus did, however, survive until almost the end of the pre-war STL operation in 1954.

Another 'survivor' to almost the end of the type was STL1867 [chassis O6614799]. This was one of the 40 vehicles built in the Spring of 1937, which had a modified design of body to suit operation through the Blackwall and Rotherhithe tunnels under the river Thames, replacing similar special NS-type buses. To give adequate clearance, a more arched roof contour was adopted and the frontal profile was more rounded than the standard STL of the period. They also did not have the roof-mounted route number box which had been adopted for the standard version from the previous Autumn. Internally, the stairs turned through a greater angle to emerge into the upper-deck gangway to gain adequate headroom and the lower-deck lost one seat at the offside rear as a result, the total capacity thus being 55, with 25 downstairs. The chassis were generally standard, though special tyres with reinforced sidewalls were fitted to withstand the continual rubbing against the kerb almost unavoidable in passing through the tunnel. The vehicle was photographed at Eltham in 1950. Later London Transport standard double-deckers were of dimensions that could pass through the tunnels, so the variant vanished.

Withdrawals of buses provided a ready supply of chassis for conversion to service vehicles of various types. London Transport produced a dozen tower wagons on former STL-class Regent chassis in 1948-49 to augment the fleet mainly on AEC goods vehicle chassis, probably with the forthcoming demise of the London tramway system particularly in mind, although the first of the batch, 722J, on chassis number 6612338 which had been STL193, one of the 60-seat vehicles placed in service by the LGOC in 1933, is seen [left] on trolleybus repair work. The crew cabs were recognisably derived from the standard STL body structure, of later origin than the original body in this case.

Other Regents were converted into various types of lorry, mostly acquiring London Transport's standard goods cab as applied to Regent or Regal chassis, not unlike a standard AEC goods vehicle cab of the late 'thirties but lower built to suit the passenger chassis. Seen above is 736J [the suffix letter J signifying Regent chassis], which was converted in 1949, using chassis 6612608, formerly STL388 of the sloping-front 1933-34 type.

However, London Transport was by no means the first to convert a Regent into a tower wagon. Nottingham Corporation decided to order a new tower wagon in 1933, choosing a Regent chassis for reasons of standardisation. When the new chassis, 6612070, arrived, it was decided to transfer the Park Royal body from one of the eight Regents delivered the previous year, No. 48 [TV 6749] to the new chassis, the resulting bus retaining the same fleet number but being registered TV 9435. The older chassis, number 6611857, was then fitted with the new tower wagon body, made by Eagle Engineering Co, and this concern also modified the chassis to 'normal' control, with driver seated behind a conventional bonnet rather than alongside the engine, thus producing what is believed to have been the only Regent of that layout. However, it appears that the steering gear may have been of the type fitted to the Ranger single-decker model of similar design. The photograph shows it engaged in tramway overhead maintenance in August 1937.

Up to 1949, London Transport could field some remarkable displays of variety. This scene, taken in the car park at Ascot race course reveals the following line-up for the special 443 service between Ascot and Staines. From left to right:- ST1128 [661156] one of the 1930 East Surrey vehicles with Ransomes body, ST509 [661790] a 1930 ex-LGOC vehicle, STL1498 [06614365] and 973 [06613261] front-entrance buses with, respectively, Weymann and LPTB bodies, ST1034 [6612023] one of the 'Bluebird' ST buses and ST993 [6611040] ex-Tilling.

[Left] Westcliff-on-Sea Motor Services Ltd was a regular AEC customer in the early 'thirties and even though Thomas Tilling Ltd acquired a controlling interest in 1935 the Regents in the fleet were in evidence until well into the post-war era. Here JN 4295 [6612731], one of a pair of vehicles with Weymann metal-framed lowbridge body-work dating from 1934 is seen in company with CHJ 254, a 1948 Bristol K5G of the standard ECW-bodied type as supplied to most Tilling companies. The Regent, despite retaining its original outline, with London-style top route number box superimposed on the typical Weymann body style, also conformed to Tilling concepts in its Gardner 5LW engine and red and cream livery. The unattractive painted radiator was quite a common feature of the period. Westcliff was taken over by Eastern National in 1955.

[Below] Brighton Hove & District was even more of a Tilling stronghold in both traditional and modern senses. No. 6335 [APM 657] on chassis O6615340, was the last Regent to be supplied to B H & D, one of a pair delivered in 1937 which were the only ones for this company [or the Tilling Brighton branch from which it took over in 1935] to have oil engines from new, 7.7-litre units being fitted. The 56-seat bodywork was originally built to virtually the same design as the London Tilling STL buses of 1932-33. In this scene in the early 'fifties, the vehicle is seen as rebuilt to incorporate some typical ECW features. The long radiator was probably original, but a typical Tilling inclined quick-acting filler had been added.

London Transport's engineers seemed to be fascinated by the concept of a double-deck Green Line coach. Despite the lack of any real success with an AEC Renown [LT1137] and an AEC Q [Q188], both six-wheelers [the latter described in 'Best of British Buses No. 2, page 82], a third attempt was made in 1948. This time it was a rebuild based on RT97 [O6616845] originally placed in service in May 1940 and an apt choice since it had an ingenious sliding entrance door that had been fitted for one of the 'Pay as you board' experiments, entering service in that form in December 1945. This experiment was a failure as was a spell in Green Line service in this form. During 1947-48, an elaborate exercise was put in hand, involving most of the bodywork and requiring removal of the radiator to a position under the stairs, where it formed part of an elaborate heating system. The front end was restyled along the lines of the 1939 TF class of Green Line coaches with a low-level and rather feature-less grille. The window pillars were slimmed down and full-depth drop windows fitted. Comfortable seats were provided for 46 passengers only, with 26 upstairs. It was completed in January 1949 and entered Green Line service in April, but by the end of the year it was demoted to country bus work and even this ceased in March 1953.

Another elaborate London Transport exercise, carried out on a much larger scale, was the rebuilding of STL-type chassis to accept RT-type bodywork. The latter was in full production by Park Royal and Weymann by 1948 and a shortage of new chassis was foreseen. However, the STL chassis required extensive alterations to conform to the RT body dimensions [which were regarded as sacrosant to maintain interchangeability], as described on page 80. The vehicles chosen for the intitial conversions were the last pre-war batch of STL buses with FJJ and FXT registrations, including STL2517 [O6616618] seen [right] at Dorking in June 1949, shortly before conversion. The completed conversions were all sent to Park Royal and emerged looking like a new RT and bearing new SRT fleet numbers, SRT 29 being seen at Arnos Grove soon after entering service in April 1949; this had been STL2576 [O6616679]. Unfortunately, what had probably been the best and certainly the most refined STL buses, with their flexibly-mounted engines, became a distinctly sub-standard RT, unpopular with drivers, and the scheme was stopped after 160 conversions had been made, including 35 using slightly earlier 1937-38 chassis. All were withdrawn by July 1954.

[Above] A possible alternative approach to what might have been done with serviceable London Transport STL chassis was represented by STL 2477, which received a new body without chassis modification in May 1950. The objective was, however, to try out a method of body construction developed by Mr A. W. Sainsbury, experimental shop foreman at Chiswick Works. It was basically of bolted construction and nicknamed the Meccano Set, although officially called the Sainsbury body. The appearance could be described as STL with traces of RT. Curiously, it was painted in the red and white livery used for obsolete or non-standard chassis, suggesting that it was not wished to make it too 'prominent'. It was retained until 1956, latterly as a staff bus.

[Below] Other operators were able to obtain long lives from the original bodywork on many of the later pre-war Regents. Leeds City Transport 274 [GUA 799] on chassis O6616054, one of 30 vehicles with 7.7-litre engines, preselective gearboxes and teak-framed Roe bodywork placed in service in 1938, looks pretty sound when photographed in the central bus station in July 1951, apart from a very slight sag in the waistrail. It was in the rather dismal early post-war blue/grey livery but still retained the 1938-type large chromium front hub cap by then becoming rather a rarity in good condition. No. 274 was withdrawn from passenger service in 1955 but retained as a driver training vehicle until 1963 when 25 years old.

Rebodying of late 'thirties Regents was not so common as with earlier examples, partly because the original bodies were often of better construction and partly because the shortage of new buses virtually ceased in the mid-'fifties. However, Glasgow Corporation was one of a number of operators following a policy of selective rebodying. The Weymann metal-bodied Regents of 1938 were not rebodied and continued in service until 1951-57. The Cowieson-bodied batch was rebodied in 1950 and renumbered, the vehicle shown here as AR 294 having been the first vehicle, No. 600 [BUS 166] with chassis O6616181. Its new 56-seat body, one of ten by Scottish Commercial, was to Crossley design. Most of these were withdrawn by 1961 but AR 294 was retained for a time as a snowplough.

[Right] Devon General obtained eighteen years service from three 8.8-litre-engined Regents with Weymann metal-framed 54-seat bodies placed in service in 1938. DR236 [ETT 997] on chassis O6615436 is seen at Paul Street bus station, Exeter, in July 1955, showing little sign of modification over the years.

[Below] Appreciably longer service was given by some of the 24 Devon General Regents with Short Bros bodywork dating from 1933-34, albeit with some modification. Half were rebodied by Brush in 1949 and the bodywork of the remainder was rebuilt between 1947 and 1951. Five of the latter vehicles were selected for conversion to open-top by Longwell Green of Bristol in 1955 and DR218 [OD 7505], on chassis O6612453, was photographed immediately afterwards. The seating capacity was increased to 55 by adding three more seats upstairs, bringing the total on that deck to 31. These five vehicles remained in service until 1961, retaining their 8.8-litre engines to the end, thus running for 27 years.

Reading Corporation standardised on Park Royal metal-framed lowbridge bodywork for its 7.7-litre Regents built in the late 'thirties which formed the major part of the fleet in the early post-war period. The last four of them, new in June 1938, survived until the end of 1958, and No. 23 [ARD 14] on chassis O6616142, is seen here earlier in the 'fifties at Reading station. These vehicles thus completed over 20 years service despite having the same form of construction that had been considered beyond economic repair on the Park Royal-bodied STL buses built in 1937 after under a dozen years.

[Above left] In 1948-49 Trent Motor Traction Co Ltd ordered the rebodying of all but one of the 30 Regent 7.7-litre buses placed in service in 1937, unusual among vehicles for a BET company in having preselective gearboxes. The new bodies were by Willowbrook and the completed vehicles were outwardly almost identical with new Regent II buses which had just entered the fleet. No. 1349 [RC 4645] on chassis O6615084 is seen here in Derby in May 1957, when 20 years old. This, like the majority of the rebuilds, was a lowbridge vehicle, having a seating capacity of 55, with 28 on the lower deck, a capacity which became common in wartime — pre-war lowbridge buses rarely exceeded 53. Only the original short radiator conveys the true age of the chassis and the overall impression of a smart vehicle was helped by Trent's simple but effective red and white livery of that period.

[Left] Nottingham City Transport No. 251 [DAU 493] on chassis O6615168 was new in November 1937, having 54-seat bodywork by Cravens Railway Carriage & Wagon Co, a make whose pre-war products were sometimes withdrawn before those of competitive bodybuilders. Yet this photograph was taken in March 1960, when the vehicle had completed over 22 years' service. The radiator blind hardly helps the appearance but the overall impression is of a sound vehicle as it heels slightly in negotiating a roundabout on its way out along the Derby Road, followed by a Northumberland-registered Rolls-Royce dating from about 1930 but evidently somewhat modernised in appearance.

AEC Regent specifications 1929–1942.

Year	1929	1930	1931	1932	1933	1934	1935	1936	1937	1938	1939	1940	1942-2
Wheelbase													
15ft. 6½in.	S	S	S	O	-	-	-	-	-	-	-	-	-
16ft. 3in.	-	-	-	O	S	S	S	S	S	S	S	S	S
Engine [all six-cylinder]													
A136 etc 100 x 130mm petrol [6.1L]	S	S	O	O	O	-	-	-	-	-	-	-	-
A145 etc 110 x 130mm petrol [7.4L]	-	O	S	-	-	-	-	-	-	-	-	-	-
A162 ditto, high power hd. [7.4L]	-	-	-	S	S	O	O	O	O	O	O	(O)	-
A155 110 x 142mm oil [8.1L]	-	-	O	-	-	-	-	-	-	-	-	-	-
A165 115 x 142mm oil [8.8L]	-	-	-	O	O	S	O	O	O	O	O	O	-
A171 105 x 146mm oil [7.7L]	-	-	-	-	L	S	S	S	O	O	O	-	-
A173 ditto, direct inj. oil [7.7L]	-	-	-	-	-	-	-	L	O	S	S	S	S
A180 115mm, direct inj. oil [8.8L]	-	-	-	-	-	-	-	-	-	O	O	O	-
Gearbox													
'Crash' [sliding-mesh]	S	S	S	-	-	-	-	-	-	-	-	-	-
'Crash' [constant-mesh 3rd]	-	-	L	S	S	S	S	S	S	S	S	S	S
Preselective [Daimler]	-	-	-	O	O	-	-	-	-	-	-	-	-
Preselective [AEC]	-	-	-	-	-	O	O	O	O	O	O	O	-
Brakes													
Vacuum-mechanical [single-servo]	S	S	-	-	-	-	-	-	-	-	-	-	-
Vacuum-mechanical [triple servo]	-	-	S	S	S	-	-	-	-	-	-	-	-
Vacuum-hydraulic [Lockheed]	-	-	-	O	O	S	S	S	S	S	S	S	S
Rear axle													
Semi-floating	S	S	S	S	-	-	-	-	-	-	-	-	-
Fully-floating	-	-	-	-	S	S	S	S	S	S	S	S	S

Key: S, Standard; O, Optional; L, Limited availability.

NOTES:

This table attempts to convey the range of standard and optional features of Regent models over the period covered by this volume. In practice there was often a degree of overlap between old and new features and some changes occurred part-way through a model year, which in any case did not generally correspond to the calendar year. A compromise has had to be struck between availability and what was actually built — an example is the theoretical availability of petrol-engined vehicles in 1940, though none were built. Experimental and 'special' models, notably the RT, are excluded.

TOTAL NUMBERS OF VEHICLES BUILT

The chassis numbers of vehicle built between 1929 and 1942 were in a sequence which began at 661001 and ran to O6617289 in a single sequence [661999 being followed by 6611000] though unfulfilled orders, mainly due to the war, meant that no vehicles were built for 89 numbers in the series, the first being 6616488.

The 'O' prefix signifying an oil-engined chassis came into use in the Autumn of 1933, the first example apparently being O6612152 a 1933 show exhibit for Reading Corporation. Gardner-engined Regents for Huddersfield and Hull had chassis numbers commencing O661G included within this series.

Of the 7200 chassis built, 5204 were of 16ft. 3in. wheelbase standardised in 1932 [though the first three were built in 1931]; all but four of the 1845 shorter 15ft. 6½in. wheelbase dating from 1932 or earlier. The balance of 151 chassis were RT type, of 16ft. 4in. wheelbase.

Approximately 2800 of the chassis were built with petrol engines and 4400 with oil, the exact figures being difficult to establish because some chassis were converted immediately after building and before entering service. Only eighteen oil-engined Regents were included in the first 2000 chassis built, but many more were converted later.

Of the total, 3674 chassis were built for LGOC [and its associated companies] or LPTB, representing 51 per cent of the total. These comprise 950 ST type [though 14 originally owned by Autocar never received ST fleet numbers], 2573 STL and 151 RT.

Daddy of all the pre-war Regents in terms of public passenger-carrying service in virtually original condition was Provincial's famous No. 35 [BOR 767], on chassis number O6614417, which entered service in 1936 and was not withdrawn until 1967, being subsequently preserved. It was one of four standard 7.7-litre chassis with Park Royal teak-framed bodywork seating 56; another of the batch, rebodied in 1955 by Reading & Co, remained in service until 1970. No. 35 is seen here as running in the late 'fifties.

Acknowledgements

Many people have helped me to write this book, often unwittingly, by adding to the storehouse of information built up during almost a lifetime's interest in the Regent, which began when I first travelled to school on some examples in 1937. More specifically and considerably more recently, I am grateful to Leyland Vehicles Ltd for access to AEC photographic archives which added significantly to the collection of photographs, official and otherwise, I had amassed.

It was a happy coincidence that Bob Smith was assisting the PSV Circle by reference to official records in compiling a list of AEC Regent chassis numbers covering precisely the period of this book — the first part, CXB81, covering numbers up to 6612070, now being complete. This helped me in filling in the remaining gaps in my own records and, conversely, I hope this book will illustrate and explain the variety of vehicles represented by the list. Members of both the PSV Circle and Omnibus Society were prominent among those who helped in my research over the years.

Others who helped with personal recollections or other background material include F. J. Sloan, Bill Jardine and Gavin Martin, all of whom were colleagues in my period with AEC in the early 'fifties. John Gillham's 32-year old booklet 'London's double-deck buses' has long been a particularly concise source of information and I must thank Gavin Booth for sending the picture of the Glasgow RT on page 75.

My usual thanks to the TPC staff at Glossop for their contribution to the finished result.

Photo Credits

Leyland Vehicles Ltd except as follows:-

G. F. Ashwell	84(top right), 87(top right)
G. H. F. Atkins	18(upper), 22(both lower), 59(centre), 74(lower) 89(bottom), 92(bottom), 93 (centre and bottom) 94(centre)
Brush Coachworks Ltd (TPC Library)	35(upper), 36(lower), 44(bottom)
J. Cull	84(top left)
B. V. Franey	91(top)
R. N. Hannay collection	66(lower), 90(bottom), 94(top)
M. L. Harper	13(lower)
W. J. Haynes	46(upper), 81(lower)
V. C. Jones	78(centre), 85(bottom)
B. Knowlman	90(top left)
G. P. B. Martin	38(bottom), 92(top)
Metro-Cammell Weymann Ltd	49(upper)
R. A. Mills	86 (all)
S. A. Newman	91(lower)
E. Ogden	93(top)
F. G. Reynolds	39(lower), 78(top), 80, 84(bottom), 88(both)
London Transport Exectuive	19, 50, 56, 70(lower), 85(top)
G. A. Rixon	91(centre)
J. A. Severn	94(bottom)
R. H. G. Simpson	74(upper), 95(bottom)
Strathclyde PTE	75(upper)
A. A. Townsin	Front cover, 87(top left)
A. A. Townsin collection	54(lower), 89(top left)
West Midlands PTE	31(lower)
P. Winding	87(bottom)
A. M. Wright	58(lower), 90(centre)